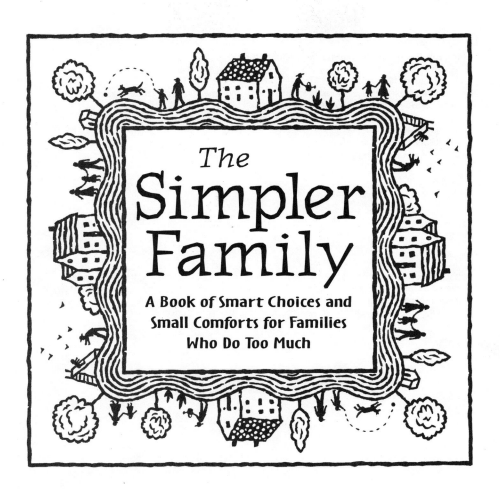

The Simpler Family

A Book of Smart Choices and Small Comforts for Families Who Do Too Much

CHRISTINE KLEIN

Robins Lane Press
a division of Gryphon House, Inc.
www.robinslane.com

Library of Congress Cataloging-in-Publication Data

Klein, Christine, 1958–.
    The simpler family: a book of smart choices and small comforts for families
who do too much / Christine Klein.
        p.   cm.
    Includes index.
    ISBN 1-58904-009-0
    1. Family—Time management.   I. Title.
HQ734.K616   2001
306.85—dc21   2001044105

Cover and interior design by Bartko Design
Cover and interior illustrations copyright © 2001 Sudi McCollum

Published by Robins Lane Press
A division of Gryphon House
10726 Tucker St., Beltsville, MD 20704 U.S.A.

With deep love and gratitude
to my simpler family:
Ed, Mackenzie and Brady
and to my parents,
Bob and Mary Lou Folzenlogen

Contents

Acknowledgements

MY SINCERE THANKS to Justin Rood of Robins Lane Press whose skillful editing, undying enthusiasm, and great sense of humor made this book much better (and more fun) than it would have been otherwise.

Preface

OUR STORY BEGINS in the spring of 1993. My husband and I had two beautiful children. Our daughter was two and a half. Our son was five months. My husband was, and still is, a high school teacher. I was a marketing director. Our combined income was $76,000. We were both satisfied with our career choices and had worked out a schedule that enabled our children to receive quality care while we attended to our jobs. My husband left for work at 6:30 A.M. each weekday. The kids and I left by 8:00 A.M. We were comfortable with the arrangements we had made for our children's care. Although the care was expensive, our combined salaries made it affordable.

In these regards, our life was perfect. In others, it was less than perfect. We were not a happy family. Our lives were a blur. Although we had worked out a schedule to accommodate everyone's needs, it required doing everything in a hurry. Each weekday morning I hurried to feed and dress each child, quickly gathered their things, and strapped them in the car. I rushed to drop them off, hoping our good-byes would be quick and cheerful so I could get to my job on time. This morning routine typically went smoothly and was not unlike the routines of my friends and coworkers. This, it seemed, was the life one could expect as the parent of young children. But it didn't feel quite right to me. Spending my weekdays at work, away from my children, in order to afford a lifestyle that I didn't especially enjoy seemed wrong, no matter how many people were doing the same thing.

We spent our weekends frantically doing all the things we needed to get done before the work week began again: grocery shopping, laundry, house and yard work, church. On Sunday evenings I sank into a mild depression. Instead of enjoying a relaxing evening with my family, I spent Sunday evenings dreading what lay beyond: another hectic week of shuffled children, frantic commutes and hurried dinners. And if I woke up Monday morning and found one of the kids too sick to go to child care, I'd try to suppress the frustration of realizing I had to forfeit another vacation day in order to stay home with my children—my husband had already left the house.

Although our everyday life slowly plodded along, it never felt right. Our children were spending most of their waking hours in someone else's care, we did everything in a hurry, and we rarely had time to relax and enjoy the life we were working so hard to afford. But because we were spending everything we earned (other than money set aside for our retirement and their college), we could not afford living without my salary . . . or so we thought.

One especially hectic morning my daughter threw a tantrum. She didn't like the way the seam of her sock felt on her toes. She refused to wear her shoes. I was frustrated and in a hurry, and I refused to spend another minute listening to her cry. I had to get to work. I crammed her shoes on her feet, threw her and her brother in the car, and we proceeded on our not-so-merry way. As she continued to whimper in the backseat, my frustration mounted until I stopped the car and screamed until my throat ached, throwing a tantrum of my own.

Eventually we arrived at the child-care center, two teary children and one defeated mom. That's when one of my daughter's warm and loving child-care providers, sensing my mood, wrapped her arms around me and assured me that things would get better.

She was right. That very day I decided this was not the life I wanted for my family. I wanted to spend less time in the car and more time at home. I wanted to stop feeling controlled by the clock and instead be controlled by the desires of myself and my family. I wanted to begin the day feeling happy and rested instead of tired and anxious. Desperate to make our lives the way we thought they should be, my husband and I looked for opportunities to modify the way we spent our time and our money. But we were sure it wouldn't be easy. We were always reasonable spenders, rarely making purchases one might consider a luxury. We lived in a modest three-bedroom home, which we planned to pay off in fifteen years. We had furnished our home with ordinary possessions, nothing especially fancy, and even equipped our children's rooms with secondhand furniture. We drove nice cars until long after they were paid for, and did not buy a lot of designer clothes or eat at expensive restaurants.

We were equally reasonable in the manner in which we spent our time. We did the laundry and cleaned the house to an acceptable level each weekend. We avoided late charges by always paying bills on time. We dutifully visited the grandparents on weekends. We even squeezed in the occasional volunteer activity. We cut down on frantic car trips and created our fondest family memories in the comfort of our own family room.

We were already so careful in the way we spent our money and our time, it was difficult to imagine we'd be able to scale back to a simpler way of life. Wasn't our life already fairly simple?

In fact, our life was already fairly simple. But it wouldn't be simple enough until our weekdays were no longer rushed, our weekends were no longer spent catching up on cleaning, laundry and grocery shopping. So we set out to look for opportunities to scale back to a simpler pattern of living. We looked for ways to spend less money, less time in the car, less time at work and less time away from our children—and from each other. The changes we made were subtle, but they were very effective. And within a few months I was able to trade my hectic full-time job for a flexible, less stressful part-time position. Our combined annual income decreased by half, but the quality of our lives increased more than I can say. My husband was happier, I was happier, my children were happier, even our dogs were happier. By simplifying our lives we became richer in ways that money could never afford.

I wrote this book for two reasons. First, because I wanted to show parents who are searching for a more meaningful family life that it is possible to have one. Second, I wanted to share what my husband and I have learned and help others avoid our mistakes. If you follow the steps outlined in this book, taking the first step will be easier, and your journey to a simpler family life will be smoother.

I hope you will carry this book with you and read it whenever you have a few spare moments. It will help you and your family begin making the choices that will lead to a simpler, happier, more fulfilling life.

Introduction

*"The Constitution only gives people the right to
pursue happiness. You have to catch it yourself."*
                                            —Ben Franklin

LIFE IS NOT A CONTEST to see who can own the biggest house,
drive the largest automobile, wear the most expensive clothes, or
hold the most impressive investment portfolio. What's most
important is how we live our life right now, and what kind of life
we give our children.

This book is not about deprivation. It's not about removing all
the luxuries from your family's life. This book is about adding
joy. It's about making smart choices regarding the way you use
your time and your money. It's about making lifestyle changes
that will enable your family to trade their hectic days for ones
that are simpler, calmer and happier.

If you implement all of the ideas in this book, you may well
find you are able to live on one income, or one and one-half
incomes. Or you may decide that both you and your spouse will
continue to work full time but return each evening to a more
peaceful, meaningful home. Everyone who reads this book will

discover that by making some changes in the way they spend their time and money, they will enjoy a richer, simpler, happier family life.

Changing to a simpler, more fulfilling family life will be possible only if you are willing to (1) examine the way you currently spend your time and money and (2) accept the challenge to change those habits.

Manufacturers desperately want us to overconsume. They want us to buy a sixteen-ounce cup of soda when an eleven-ounce cup is more than enough. They spend billions of dollars convincing us that we can't live without their newest invention. How did we ever survive without aromatherapy? Or fifty-seven kinds of breakfast cereal?

Every day we make choices about how to spend our money—money that we have worked long hours away from our families to obtain. Some of our choices involve a sizeable amount of our hard-earned cash. Do we buy the Land Rover with all the extras, buy a new minivan instead, or settle for a used station wagon? Many of our choices are smaller. Do we rent a movie at Blockbuster? Two movies? New or old release? Buy a box of Raisinettes? Do I pack my lunch or go out with coworkers?

Every chapter of this book will encourage you to reconsider the choices you make in your daily life and to exercise your power as a consumer to refuse the luxuries, the add-ons and the "conveniences" that are ultimately taking you away from your family. You'll also be asked to examine your use of time. Do you plan in advance, or do you exist on spur-of-the-moment decisions that aren't always best for your family?

By scaling back to a simpler way of life, your family will be rewarded in ways you might never have imagined. Here are some of the biggest benefits you'll soon enjoy:

More Control of Time and Money

You will remove all the extraneous activities that complicate daily life and have time to enjoy every day with your family, not just the weekends or family vacations. You'll no longer live for the future, the weekend or the next holiday. Instead, you'll be able to appreciate the here and now.

Instead of allowing other people and demands to schedule your day, you will find the strength to say, "No, I don't want to go to that baby shower, PTA meeting, Tupperware party, financial seminar." You will have other plans. You will have planned to stay home with your family, to enjoy your home, the day, the moment.

Your family will rediscover the utter joy of lying in the warm sun on a chilly day, or in the cool shade of a tree on a warm day, escaping within the pages of a good book. You'll relive the dizzy sensation of lying very still in the grass watching the clouds drift by. You'll stand at your kitchen window grinning as you watch your kids organize the whole neighborhood in a game of hide-and-go-seek. And you'll go to bed at night fully content at the thought of having spent an entire day enjoying your family and home.

Less Stress, Better Sleep, More Exercise

Out-of-control spending, frantic commutes and sleepless nights are bad habits of a not-so-simple lifestyle. These habits cause undue stress, that is, the "wear and tear" our bodies experience as we adjust to a continuously changing environment.

Eliminating stress is one of the biggest benefits of a simpler family life. Instead of the need to recover from a stressful day at work in front of the television, you'll be ready to take a walk, ride a bike or play a game of basketball with the kids. And because less stress and more exercise is a common cure for insomnia, your new lifestyle will improve your sleep habits. You'll awake feeling rested and full of energy. The restless nights, irritable days and resulting health problems will disappear.

Healthier Eating Habits

Perhaps you've always wanted to prepare more nutritious meals for your family and to pack nutritious lunches for your kids instead of having them buy the school lunch. But you never had time to pull it all together.

A simplified work and family schedule will provide the time and energy you need to accomplish both. You'll finally be able to make healthy changes in everyone's diet.

You might even find yourself preparing sandwiches or salads made with vegetables grown in your own backyard garden. There certainly is a higher level of enjoyment that comes from eating homegrown fruits and vegetables for lunch versus opening a cellophane package of precut bologna and cheese. You'll say good-bye to dinners on the fly. Instead of a fast-food dinner in the car on the way to your child's next sports practice, you'll enjoy family dinners around your own kitchen table. Perhaps a prayer of thanksgiving for your renewed sense of family, your good health, and your time together will become a regular part of your meal.

More Involvement in Your Children's Education

With a new, simplified lifestyle you will be able to spend more time helping your children learn and be successful in school. You'll have time to review homework each evening, help them study for important tests, and ensure steady progress toward major projects. With your help, your children will be well prepared for the following day.

You may even have time to periodically volunteer at school, which will let you get to know teachers, staff and classmates. Your children may be more successful in school as a result. Based on a 1994 study, the U.S. Department of Education found that family involvement in children's education is closely linked to children's school success.

More Time to Evaluate Career Goals

As you ease the frantic pace of your life, you will soon enjoy a more peaceful, open frame of mind. Without all the pulling and tugging of your former hectic days, you'll gradually open your eyes to a world of career opportunities. Search for a career that you love, and eventually you'll know exactly what you want to do with your life.

More Environmental Awareness

Families that choose a simpler lifestyle tend to develop an appreciation for our Earth's resources and a desire to preserve them. Recycling and conserving will become ways of life for your family. Your family will thrill at the idea of eating foods grown in your own garden, nurtured with rich compost that has resulted from your kitchen and yard waste. You'll hesitate before throwing usable items in the trash, choosing instead to recycle.

More Consumer Consciousness

As you happily adjust to a simpler way of life, your level of personal consumption will drop significantly. You will find yourself watching television commercials and wondering how anyone could think one particular brand is superior over another simply because a football superstar says it is. You'll shake your head in wonder at the parents who buy prepackaged brownies with do-it-yourself blue icing and sprinkles for $1.75 a piece for their children's lunches. And you'll question the sensibility of anyone who would purchase a $40,000 gas-guzzling SUV.

As you may have observed, people tend to spend money when they are unhappy. You will no longer be counted among them. The happier you become at home, the less will be your desire for unnecessary spending. An afternoon of playing tag, baking or reading with your children will magically erase your need for a new pair of running shoes or sweater.

The move to a simpler family is within reach if you are willing to take the steps outlined in this book. The alternative is to do what you're doing for the rest of your life. The choice is yours.

CHAPTER 1

Organization

"Everyone is complaining of being tired, of not having time for what they wish to do . . . It would be a wonderful relief if, by eliminating both wisely and well, life might be simplified."

—Laura Ingalls Wilder

YOU CAN ACCOMPLISH a lot more with a lot less if you are well organized. It's true of money, space, time—just about anything. In fact, all the benefits of a simpler life outlined in this book stem from a family that is well organized. The theme resounds in every chapter.

Once you're a well-organized family, you won't miss important events, you won't forget to pay a bill, you won't be running out at the last minute for a birthday gift or for a can of chicken broth. Instead, you'll gather around the table together for home-made meals. You'll have time to organize neighborhood volley-ball games or backyard barbecues. You'll spend weekends hanging around the house with the kids. And you'll celebrate holidays the way they were meant to be celebrated.

Implement just some of the ideas that follow and you'll find yourself spending less time on activities that have little meaning (like housework and paying bills), and more time on activities the family enjoys.

Organizing Your Time

Most families have countless demands on their time. Many of these demands are routine. We barely think about why we do them. We just do them. Your friends, family and coworkers are all good at adding to your to-do list. Have any of them ever recommended crossing something off? If you are ever to eliminate a demand for your time, it is up to you to make that decision. Remember, the shorter your to-do list, the more time you have to relax and have fun. You are also the one to decide if taking on a new responsibility will get you closer to your dream of a simpler life.

Many people, myself included, have a hard time saying no. Here's a solution: the next time someone asks for a slice of your valuable free time, say, "I'll need to check and get back to you." This will give you the chance to think it over and decide if it's important enough (or fun enough) to fit into your schedule.

To scale back to a more simplified life, examine the things that are filling your life right now. Start by making a list of all the demands for your time that you face in the coming week. Determine how each activity fits with your goal of a more simplified life by asking yourself the following questions:

- Am I doing something because everyone else is, or because my mother or father used to?
- Are my kids involved in an activity because they really want to be involved, or because their friends are?
- Is the family benefiting from the activity, or could we derive the same benefits from an activity done together at home?
- Am I doing something only because I think it is expected of me?
- Which of these activities matter the most to my family?
- Am I doing it only because I will feel guilty if I don't?

Your answers to these questions will help you determine, on a case-by-case basis, if each activity is worthy of your precious free time. After asking ourselves these questions, my husband and I made the following changes:

- *Drive kids to and from sports practices.* First, we questioned whether our kids were involved in too many activities. (See Chapter 5 for more on this subject.) For those activities we did not eliminate, we arranged car pools whenever possible. On days when it was our turn to drive, we bundled the trip with something else we wanted to accomplish, like getting in exercise while waiting for practice to end.
- *Bake cupcakes for the Parent Teacher Organization bake sale.* When my kids first started school, I baked for nearly every school

event, at least one activity per month. I finally decided that once a year was sufficient.

- *Plan and teach Sunday school class.* After years of teaching Sunday school, it occurred to me that most other parents weren't doing their part. Now I teach the first eight-week session and let other parents do their fair share the rest of the school year.
- *Schedule family checkups.* While taking our son to the dentist for a checkup, we wondered, What about the rest of the family? Whenever possible, we now arrange for everyone to have their checkups at the same time.
- *Buy multiple birthday gifts.* All children get invited to a half-dozen birthday parties a year. We saved ourselves valuable time by finding a gift our child approved of and buying five of them when they were on sale. You may prefer to make gifts in advance instead, like bubble bath or stationery (see Chapter 6.)

The Two-Calendar System

Even after paring down your to-do list, you will probably still have lots of activities to juggle in the course of a month. You can keep track of them all with a two-calendar system. It's simple to implement and will ensure you never miss an appointment or deadline.

Master Calendar

Get an inexpensive twelve-month calendar that will fit inside the door of your kitchen cabinet that is closest to the phone. This will keep it out of sight but still easy to access when you're making plans on the phone. On this calendar, fill in every doctor and dentist appointment, birthday, and important once-a-year event like a dance recital, SAT test, graduations, vacations, and household maintenance items (see Chapter 4).

Vacations can include lots of deadlines that should all be noted on your Master Calendar: renew passports, make reservations at a kennel, call to stop your newspaper and mail. Do not clutter this calendar with routine activities like sports practices and games. You'll keep track of them elsewhere.

Once the year has ended, do not throw the calendar away. You'll want to refer to it during tax time, as the mileage to and from doctor's appointments is deductible, and to transfer birthday and anniversary dates to your new calendar.

Monthly Activity Calendar

This second calendar will guarantee you won't miss an appointment, forget the car pool, or pay a late fee on library books, ever. It's like a day planner for the entire family, but it's much larger, and you won't carry it with you.

Buy a large (seventeen-by-twenty-two-inch) monthly desk pad calendar at an office supply store. (Or find a large piece of blank paper each month and make your own calendar.) These calendars have nice big blocks of space for every day of the month. Tear off the sheet that corresponds to the upcoming month.

Fill this calendar with every activity your family has. Pull out all activity schedules and school memos and transfer all the information for the month onto this large calendar. Next, look at your Master Calendar and transfer relevant information. Keep a pencil nearby, as you will add to the calendar throughout the month. Your calendar should include the following:

- Sports practices and games
- Deadlines for homework projects
- Due dates for library books and videos
- Parties
- Meetings
- Birthdays
- Due dates for major bills (Mark your calendar for a week before the bill is actually due to avoid a late charge.)
- Volunteer projects
- Car pools (Note when it is your turn to drive.)

This calendar should hang on the side of your refrigerator or another location in the kitchen, close to the phone. Get in the habit of checking it each evening as you plan the next day. You will never again pay a late fee at the library or forget carpool duty if you keep this calendar updated and refer to it daily.

Once-a-Year Scheduling

Scheduling doctor and dental checkups at a time convenient for the family can be difficult. You decide Friday is best, only to find the dentist doesn't have a Friday appointment available for the next two months. Avoid such hassles by making all appointments a year at a time. In December, as you're preparing your new Master Calendar, make a year's worth of appointments with the doctor, dentist, gynecologist, hair stylist, dog groomer, and other hard-to-schedule people. You can always reschedule if necessary.

Getting it on your calendar will ensure such important appointments won't be forgotten.

Lists! Lists! Lists!

Once I had children, my ability to remember a long list of things vanished. On a day when I was set to run a half-dozen errands, I'd get in the car, make it to the first four places, and return home befuddled because I couldn't remember those last two things I wanted to do. Now, before I leave the house, I jot down a list of each of the places I need to stop, arranging the list in the most logical order. It's a simple time-saver.

Housework vs. Playtime

Scheduling playtime can ensure your free time isn't consumed with less-rewarding activities. Like most moms, my girlfriend Mary has a hard time relaxing at home when there is laundry or other housework to be done. So on the weekends she makes it a point to take her son to the park. "If we stay home, I end up doing housework, and he ends up playing with his friends. Going to the park gives us the opportunity to play alone with no distractions."

Organizing Your Finances

Paying Bills

Everyone seems to have his or her own unique system for paying and filing bills. Most people I know pile their bills in a designated spot. Every couple of weeks they go through them, paying those that will soon be due. After paying bills, they file all receipts. To keep the process simple, here is what I recommend:

- Open the bill as it arrives and write the due date on the outside of the envelope.
- For bills that carry a hefty late fee (credit cards), jot a reminder on your monthly activity calendar for a week before the actual due date. This will assure you get the bill paid on time.
- Keep unpaid bills in a specific location, away from other mail and paperwork.
- Every two weeks, glance at the due date, which you have written on the outside of the envelopes, and pay anything that is due soon.
- Once paid, file the statements for credit cards and utilities. Discard all other statements unless you have a reason for hanging onto them. As you prepare your tax return, you'll need to refer to these statements, so be sure to keep them in an orderly fashion.

My sister has her own simple method of bill payment. She pays all bills by phone with a credit card. This saves on checks, envelopes and postage. As soon as the bill arrives in the mail she phones the company, gives them her credit card number, then immediately throws the bill away. She keeps only the statements for her credit card bills and canceled checks, so she is never faced with a stack of statements to be filed. In her twenty years of marriage she has never once had the need to refer to an old bill.

I know of others who arrange in advance to have all bills deducted from their checking account, or automatically billed to their credit card. The phone company, for example, will deduct their charges directly from their customer's checking account, then send the customer a receipt as a reminder of the transaction. This paperless way of paying bills is certainly a time-saver. But some banks charge for the debit service, so investigate first before making such arrangements.

Shopping for a Bank

As mentioned, some banks charge their customers for debit services. Others charge for ATM usage, for not maintaining a minimum balance, or for too many transactions in a month. If you don't check closely, you may have fees withdrawn from your account without even realizing it. Find out what fees your bank imposes on its customers. Then compare those fees against other banks. It may pay to switch.

Saving Receipts

You make a purchase. Two days later the item breaks. You go to return it. Where's the receipt? Make returns quick and easy by getting in the habit of placing all receipts in a special container. We use a jar inside the kitchen cabinet and periodically toss out old receipts.

Tracking Expenses

Keeping track of your expenses and living within a predetermined budget are key to scaling back to a lifestyle that includes less time at work and more time with family. In Chapter 9 you'll learn how to track your expenses and establish a budget. Doing so will help you realize where your money is currently being spent and what adjustments you can make to get you closer to your goal of a simpler lifestyle.

Organizing Your Paperwork

Piles of mail, bills, and school papers can be disruptive and a time-waster. Instead of allowing piles to stack up, taking valuable counter or table space, get in the habit of putting each piece in its proper place as soon as you look at it. Immediately discard junk mail. Stack bills in a cabinet or basket until paid. Decide what other papers are important, and deal with them accordingly. Learning to deal with paperwork as it arrives is important to a simplified household.

School Papers

Once my kids started school, they came home with lots of important papers that couldn't be thrown away: school discipline policy, instructions from the choir teacher, bus passes. After losing a few important papers and spilling coffee on others, I got organized. I found a large manila envelope for each child and put the child's name on the front. All important papers pertaining to that child are placed in his or her envelope, including sports schedules, notes from teachers, and information about special school events. Envelopes are kept in the kitchen next to the cookbooks. As a new school year begins, all papers from the previous school year are discarded. We haven't lost an important paper since implementing this idea.

Piles of Mail

Although you unfortunately can't cancel your mail like you can the newspaper, you are able to limit the amount of time you deal with it. My friend Mary picks up her mail just a few times a week instead of every day. This reduces the amount of time she spends sorting out the junk mail from the more important pieces. In an era of E-mail, voice mail and faxes, truly time-sensitive information doesn't come in your mailbox anymore.

The typical family of four receives 500 pieces of advertising mail each year, 200 of them catalogs. Every time you enter a contest, make a donation, subscribe to a magazine or send in a warranty card, your name and address are added to another mailing list that is rented, sold or traded to another advertiser or catalog publisher.

If you receive catalogs you don't want, do one or more of the following:

1. Phone the company that sent it and ask that your name be removed from its mailing list. They may need the customer number from the mailing label, so have the catalog with you when making the call.

2. When corresponding with companies, write, "do not rent/sell my name" near the space where you fill in your name and address.

3. Write to the following clearinghouse, and ask that your name be removed from all mailing lists. Send your name in every variation shown on the junk mail you receive, and include your signature as authorization: Mail Preference Service,

Direct Marketing Association, P.O. Box 9008, Farmingdale, NY 11735-9008.

School Projects

As soon as their first child starts preschool, parents are deluged with masterpiece art projects on a daily basis. What to do with all these masterpieces quickly becomes a problem. My friend Mary strung a clothesline near the ceiling of her kitchen and used clothespins to hang artwork created by her three little ones. As a new piece was hung, an old piece was discarded.

I recommend keeping a large basket somewhere in the house to temporarily hold the work that is too new to be thrown away. If a piece is extra special, it can be displayed on the refrigerator or bulletin board for a short time. Eventually all masterpieces end up in the trash unless it meets the following criteria:

- It deserves framing (see Chapter 4).
- It deserves to be placed in the family's Memory Box. This box holds carefully selected mementos that you can't bear to discard (pacifier, lock of baby hair, Easter bonnet). Keep the box safely stored in a closet, high enough so little ones can't get to it.

Organizing Your House

Kitchen

Rarely do we look at a room with a fresh eye and consider rearranging things to make the room more efficient. But nowhere could this exercise save you more time than in the kitchen.

Because we spend so much time in our kitchens (where does everyone gather when you have a party?), it seems to become home for more things than are actually necessary. Are you using valuable shelf space for gadgets you never use? Is the top of your refrigerator packed with things that could be stored in cabinets instead—if there was room?

Open every cabinet in your kitchen and search for items you rarely, or never, use. These are some items we found:

- Wok
- Juicer
- Salad spinner
- Food dehydrator
- Waffle iron
- More pots and pans than we could possibly use to prepare a meal
- Special cutting knives
- Plastic cups from kids' meals and sporting events (and accompanying crazy straws)
- More coffee mugs than we'll ever use
- Vegetable steamer
- Egg poacher
- More margarine tubs than we'll ever need
- Cappuccino maker

For a cleaner, simpler, more efficient kitchen, store only what you regularly use. Put everything else in the basement or attic. After three months, if you haven't missed it, get rid of it. The same goes for cookbooks, recipes and quirky ingredients hiding in the far reaches of your cabinets. Use your newfound cabinet space to store items currently stored on top of the refrigerator or counter. Your kitchen will look much simpler without all the clutter, and preparing meals will be accomplished more quickly.

Outdoor Grill

We have a gas grill outside on our deck and use it year-round. Rain, snow, blazing heat—it doesn't matter. We like the taste of grilled food and like the fact that it simplifies kitchen cleanup even more. Be sure to pull your grill away from the house before using it, even in the rain or snow, in order to prevent the heat from scorching your house. Keeping your grill clean between frequent uses is simple: when finished grilling, close the lid and turn the burners on high for ten minutes. This will burn off any food that may have stuck to the grates or dripped onto the briquettes. To ensure the briquettes stay clean, periodically turn them over, and operate the grill on high with the lid closed for ten minutes. Before grilling, get in the habit of spraying grates with nonstick cooking spray.

Chapter 2 includes lots of organizational ideas to simplify your grocery shopping and meal preparation.

Housework

When I was pregnant with my first child, I asked an older, experienced mom if she had any advice. Her response: "When my children were young, I wish I had worried less about keeping the house clean and more about spending time with them." I have never forgotten her honest reply.

If, like me, you're not eager to do any more house- and yard-work than is necessary. I recommend you put the family on a schedule like the one here. This schedule was designed for a family of four but can be accommodated to any size family. In addition to the chores listed, everyone is responsible for making his or her bed and keeping his or her room clean.

	Mom	Dad	Child, Age 10	Child, Age 8
Monday	prepare dinner	dishes	set table, one load of laundry	clear table, make lunches
Tuesday	dishes	prepare dinner	set table, make lunches	clear table, take out garbage
Wednesday	prepare dinner	dishes	set table, one load of laundry	clear table, make lunches
Thursday	dishes	prepare dinner	set table, make lunches	clear table, sweep kitchen floor
Friday	prepare dinner	dishes	set table	clear table
Saturday	dust	vacuum	one load of laundry	stack wood, sweep front porch
Sunday	dishes	prepare dinner	set table, make lunches	clear table

Some parents like to change the kids' chores from week to week. I prefer keeping it the same for at least two months at a time. That way, if a chore hasn't been done, I automatically know whom to remind.

Rather than "assign" chores, try to get each family member to "choose" the chores he or she most prefers. No one family member should be unfairly burdened with more than his or her fair share. Keep the attitude "we're in this together," and expect everyone to contribute to a comfortable environment.

Don't underestimate your children's capabilities. Any child old enough to walk can carry dirty dishes to the sink. Three-year-olds can pick up toys, sort socks and attempt to make their beds. Ten-year-olds can be taught to do the laundry. Teach your children to help you, and they will rise to your expectations.

Many parents have shared their housecleaning ideas with me. They are all designed to keep housekeeping to a minimum—you have more important things to do. Here are some ideas I especially like:

- *Make a weekly housecleaning checklist.* Assign chores for every day of the week. If you stick to the schedule, your house is always clean and ready for unexpected guests. The kids are in charge of making their own beds and keeping their rooms straightened. The list looks something like this:

  Monday: clean bathrooms, vacuum
  Tuesday: dust, clean all mirrors
  Wednesday: laundry, vacuum
  Thursday: change sheets

Friday: clean kitchen floor, wipe down cabinets and refrigerator

Saturday: laundry, vacuum

- *Make it easy to keep things off the floor.* Put pegs or hooks inside the door you use most often, as well as in the kitchen and the kids' bedrooms. Insist that coats, hats, umbrellas and dog leashes all get hung, not dropped on the floor. Toys with lots of pieces can be kept in fabric tote bags and hung in bedrooms.

- *Have kids remove their shoes when they enter the house.* My friend with the white kitchen floor started this routine when she discovered how difficult it was to keep the floor clean for more than an hour. Place a nice basket at the door to keep shoes from disappearing under the couch.

- *Sort dirty laundry as it is collected.* My sister, whose home has all bedrooms on the top floor, keeps two laundry baskets in a hall closet. Everyone sorts their clothes by lights and darks. When a basket gets full, it's time to do the laundry.

- *After your kids have cleaned their rooms, check the hamper.* Sometimes they'll find it easier to stuff clean clothes in the hamper rather than putting them back in the drawer or closet. If your children are guilty, carefully explain to them the time and expense associated with washing and drying clothes. Chapter 8 outlines such expenses. While you're at it, remind them that it's OK to wear the same outfit more than once before laundering.

- *Sort clean laundry by bedroom.* Keep an empty laundry basket near the dryer for every bedroom in the house. As clothes come out of the dryer, place them in the appropriate basket. When children need clean clothes, they know where to look. Make it their job to put their clean clothes away and return the empty basket to the dryer.

- *Keep cleaning supplies on every level.* Keep dust cloths and supplies on each level of your home, and the dusting will get completed much more frequently. The same goes for window cleaning supplies. Don't own two vacuums? Put a vacuum on your "wish list" (see Chapter 6), or look for one at a yard sale.

- *Practice a professional cleaner's vacuum secrets.* I visited a friend's home just as her cleaning crew was preparing to leave. The just-vacuumed family room smelled fresh, not like the dusty smell I sometimes get after vacuuming. Their secrets? Empty the vacuum bag whenever it is half full; keep the vacuum rollers and belts clean; when changing bags, spritz your favorite fragrance on a cotton ball and then put the ball inside the bag. The fragrance will fill the room every time you vacuum.

- *Keep wall decorations simple.* Have you ever visited someone's home where every inch of wall space is covered with decorations? It can look very charming, but I wouldn't want to clean it. One nice piece of artwork above the couch or fireplace can be more attractive, and much easier to clean, than an eclectic collection. The same applies to shelving. Dusting the mantle takes only seconds if you have just one or two items to move, as opposed to a dozen pictures and knickknacks.

- *Make housecleaning enjoyable.* Put on your favorite dance music, and inform everyone that they must clean until the music stops. This can make dusting the living room a lot more fun.

Just be careful not to knock over a lamp with one of your clever dance moves.

- *Remember—the less "stuff" you have, the less you have to clean.* Remind yourself of this the next time you see something you think you can't live without.

- *Cleaning expert Don Aslett offers this advice: Avoid the "highs-and-lows" style of housekeeping.* One week you're in a cleaning frenzy; the next week the dirt doesn't bother you, so it just piles up. Instead, establish an acceptable cleanliness level and maintain it. To do so requires learning to wipe down shower walls and plumbing fixtures daily. You'll wipe up spills immediately, when it's easier, faster, and much less damaging than if you put it off.

- *Hire a cleaning service.* Although it costs fifty dollars a visit, my friend Mary considers her every-other-week cleaning service a necessary luxury. They dust, vacuum, change sheets, unload and load the dishwasher, wash the floors, clean the bathrooms and dust baseboards and above doors. "It is such a relief to know I don't have to clean anything on a regular basis," she says.

- *Remind yourself that household dirt never killed anybody.* The next time the kids ask you to play Go Fish, put down the dust rag, and enjoy your children.

Anticipate Your Needs

Once your family is well organized, you'll learn to plan in advance, anticipating your future needs before they become critical, and costly. Buying a birthday present on the way to the party is almost always more costly and stressful than purchasing one in advance. Selecting and purchasing a new lawn mower in one afternoon will cost more in stress and money than buying one after looking for a replacement at the end of the previous summer. Discovering your child needs a new winter coat on the day the thermometer hits twenty will send you rushing to the store, regardless of previous plans to relax at home.

Spur-of-the-moment purchases are costly in terms of money, time and stress. Anticipate your future needs, and enjoy the relaxation that results.

The Needs Notebook

If you've ever found yourself rushing to the department store for a pair of boots just hours after the year's first snowfall, or if you ended the summer with zero pair of swim goggles (even though you began the summer with four), you'll save time and money in the future by keeping a "Needs Notebook." This small notebook, stored in your car's glove compartment, will keep your list of the things your family needs before the season is upon you again. When you notice at the end of the winter that your children's sleds are falling apart, write it in the Needs Notebook. They are sure to be on sale in March or April.

In addition to listing items you'll need in the future, list your family's clothing sizes in your notebook. As you shop yard sales, consignment stores and the mall, bring your notebook with you. The next time you see an item at a price you can't afford to pass up, check your notebook. If it's on your list, by all means, make the purchase. If it's not on the list, skip it. You won't buy what you don't need, and you will get great off-season savings on items you do need.

The Ever-Ready Duffel

Sports activities all require some type of equipment. Get your children in the habit of anticipating what they'll need for their next practice. Give them a duffle or tote bag specifically for that activity. Then, when you're running late for swim practice, just grab the swim duffel, and you're off. My daughter has dance class every Monday after school. Before leaving for school Monday morning, or Sunday evening, it is her responsibility to put her dance duffle (with shoes, leotard and tights) in my car. We go straight from school to dance class, always prepared.

Major Purchases

Significant money can be saved by anticipating major purchases like appliances, vehicles and furniture. If your car is eight years old and acting up, start looking for a replacement before it completely dies. If you'll need a new kitchen table and chairs within the next year, start looking at new or secondhand furniture stores now. The great deal you may find today on a kitchen set will surely not be available six months from now when you are desperate. If you're thinking of flying somewhere for your vacation nine months from now, finalize your plans and shop for airline tickets now. Chapter 8 provides more ideas for spending less on major expenses.

CHAPTER 2

Food

"Life is what's happening while we're busy making other plans."

—Unknown

WHETHER AT THE kitchen table, at the neighborhood diner, on a blanket in the park, or in the backseat of the car, we nourish our bodies with food several times a day. Food is central to our lives. To a busy family, the act of buying, preparing and eating food can be time-consuming and frustrating. But it doesn't have to be. If you simplified your shopping, your meals, and your expectations of what you and your children need to consume in a day's time, your food would cost significantly less, take less

23

time to purchase and prepare, be more nutritious, taste as good or better and add joy to the end of your busy day.

The process of simplifying your food involves several steps. The payoff for your family makes each step well worth the effort, as you will discover.

Saving Time Grocery Shopping

It has been proved over and over again that the more time you spend in a supermarket, the more money you spend. In fact, a store's layout is designed to get you to spend as much time in the store as possible. That's why many grocers offer a free cup of coffee as you enter. They want you to meander your way through the aisles, sipping your hot java, as you fill your cart with items you hadn't intended to buy.

According to the trade magazine Progressive Grocer, the average shopping trip in 1995 lasted 52.9 minutes. With a little organization, you can shop for a week's worth of groceries in one-third of the time. Much of the advice that follows is aimed at reducing the amount of time you spend grocery shopping. It may seem like a lot of work, and it is at first. But once you do your homework, you will spend much less time and money at the grocery store, and you'll spend much more time with your family.

The Master Grocery List

Before a simpler lifestyle took hold in our home, my husband and I made three or four trips to the grocery store each week.

It was frustrating. We went with a list of things we had jotted down during the days prior. But once we returned home, we inevitably discovered something we needed that hadn't been put on the list.

Once we had children, we simply didn't have the time or the energy to make so many trips to the grocery store. That's when we developed a master grocery list. This is a list of every grocery item we typically buy in a two-week period. Once the list was complete, we rewrote it in the order that the items appear in the grocery store. That means the first item on our list is the first item we would come to as we entered the store . . . and so on. Once we started using the list, we discovered three things:

1. We made fewer trips to the store. That's because before we leave the house, we check our stock of each item on the list. When we get back home, we no longer realize we forgot something.

2. We spent less time in the store. Now we spend about twenty minutes doing a week's worth of shopping. When your list is in aisle order, you don't wander back and forth throughout the store in search of things you missed, increasing the possibility of grabbing other items you don't need.

3. We had a smaller grocery bill. We zip in and out so fast that we are much less apt to notice the special promotions posted throughout the store, intended to slow you down and get you to buy things you really don't need.

Here's our master grocery list:

Master Grocery List

Carrots	Graham crackers	Foil/plastic wrap
Potatoes	Peanut butter	Sandwich bags
Onions	Jelly	Napkins
Applesauce	Ketchup	Shampoo
Apple juice	Coffee	Toothpaste
Canned pears	Cooking oil	Aspirin
pineapple	Shortening	Taco chips
peaches	Cereal—generic	Pretzels
Canned vegetables	Chex	Ground turkey
Milk	Cheerios	Ice cream
Yogurt	Rice Krispies	Bread: white and
Cheese: cheddar	Kix	wheat
mozzarella	Lunch meat	Buns: hot dog and
Eggs	Chicken	hamburger
Margarine	Ground beef	**Other:**
Cinnamon rolls	Paper towels	Apples
Spaghetti sauce	Laundry detergent	Bananas
Noodles	Dishwasher	Salad dressing
Tuna	detergent	Tissue
Soup	Dishwashing liquid	Diet pop
Saltines	Bleach	

In the bottom right corner of our list is a section marked "Other." These are items we buy at another store because we know we can get a better price or improved quality than at the store where we typically shop.

Once you've completed your master grocery list, make lots of copies, and hang one on the refrigerator at all times. Throughout the week, when you realize you need something, simply circle it on the list (or jot it in its appropriate spot if it's not a part of the list). When it's time to go shopping, you know just what you need.

Taking Inventory

Once you simplify your lifestyle, you'll have a freezer stocked with leftovers and items you purchased in bulk when the price was too good to pass up. Inside a kitchen cabinet, keep an inventory of what's in your freezer. This will make it easy to plan meals in advance, virtually eliminating the last-minute decision to eat out because there is nothing in the house.

Preparing Last-Minute Meals

Keep the ingredients for your family's two favorite meals on hand at all times. This also prevents any last-minute, expensive trips for fast food.

Meal Planning

Before leaving for the grocery store, plan your meals for the week. Make sure your list includes every item you'll need to prepare this week's worth of meals. A week in advance may seem a little rigid, but it guarantees you'll have all the ingredients you need for the week, eliminating trips to the store for the items you forgot. A last-minute run to the nearest grocery store for a thirty-nine-cent can of tomato paste can easily turn into an eight-dollar purchase: you enter the store and notice the strawberries look delicious, even though they're out of season and priced sky-high. But they taste great on shortbread with whipped cream, which just happens to be strategically placed in the produce section next to the strawberries.

Comparing Prices

The day I quit my full-time job was a wake-up call for me. I knew our grocery bill could be reduced. But I didn't know how much of a reduction was possible until I did some serious price comparisons.

In a notebook, make a list of items your family commonly uses each week. Across the top list several stores, including the store where you usually shop. With notebook, calculator and pencil in hand, spend the day on a mission: to find the store with the most inexpensive prices. Here are some rules to ensure fair comparisons:

- *Include a warehouse club on your comparison-shopping trip.* Although they often require bulk purchases, or their containers are much larger than you'd prefer, compare their prices anyway. If you discover this store has the best prices of all, you may figure out a storage solution. (A case of peanut butter under the bed never hurt anybody.) During your visit, ask if the store has an annual membership fee.

- *Include stores that are outside your neighborhood if they might have better prices.* The store we now shop is ten miles from our home. And it is one we had never set foot in before my comparison-shopping trip.
- *Forget about brand names.* If peanut butter is on your list, look for the most inexpensive peanut butter in each store. If, later, you decide that the cheaper brand isn't tasty enough for your family, you can always switch back to a more expensive brand (but I bet you won't).
- *To make fair comparisons, note the size as well as the price of each item.* Then compare the prices ounce for ounce, rather than item for item.
- *Ignore sale prices.* You want to compare the price the store normally charges for an item, not a one-time sale price.

I hoped to find that one store had the lowest prices on every single item. But because I didn't want to be shopping at several stores each week, I had decided we could pay more for one or two items if the overall bill at one store was significantly lower. Here's a sample of what I found:

Item	Save-a-Lot	Kroger	Sam's Warehouse Club	IGA
Diced tomatoes	.027/oz	.035/oz	.032/oz	.048/oz
Creamy peanut butter	.072/oz	.10/oz	.088/oz	.088/oz
Chunk pineapple in juice	.04/oz	.055/oz	.042/oz	.06/oz
Applesauce	.032/oz	.044/oz	.035/oz	.037/oz
Light tuna in water	.055/oz	.13/oz	.075/oz	.13/oz
Milk, 2 percent	2.69/gal	2.89/gal	2.27/gal	2.89/gal

After comparing prices ounce per ounce, determine how much a typical shopping trip would cost if you purchase only these items. Here's what I found for my sample items:

Item	Save-a-Lot	Kroger	Sam's Warehouse Club	IGA
Diced tomatoes, 29 oz	.78	1.02	.93	1.39
Peanut butter, 36 oz	2.59	3.60	3.17	3.17
Chunk pineapple, 40 oz	1.60	2.20	1.68	2.40
Applesauce, 50 oz	1.60	2.20	1.75	1.85
Light tuna in water, 36 oz	1.98	4.75	2.70	4.75
Milk, 2 percent one gallon	2.69	2.89	2.27	2.89
Total	**$11.24**	**$16.66**	**$12.50**	**$16.45**

Based on the results, we decided to do the bulk of our shopping at Save-a-Lot. Although it is ten miles from our home, we think the savings are worth it.

After you complete your comparison-shopping trip, save your notebook. Keep it in a convenient spot. The next time you see an ad for something you typically buy, check the notebook to see if the advertised price is really cheaper than what you're already paying. Soon you'll be a well-informed, powerful consumer, acutely aware of the price for every food item you buy.

Stocking the Freezer

If you have the space, a second freezer can be a real money (and time-) saver. It lets you stock up on foods when they are priced their lowest and store fruits and vegetables from your garden. And if you know other gardeners, you'll never again turn down their bumper crop of zucchini, tomatoes or other produce they can't keep. You'll also have the room to stock up on meat when it goes on sale.

With a second freezer, you can prepare lots of meals in advance. Just double the recipe for dinners on nights when you're starting from scratch, then freeze half of it. This is not a license to spend madly at every Tupperware party in town. Instead, use those empty margarine tubs. Stick a piece of masking tape on the side, and use permanent marker to indicate the contents and the date you put it in the freezer. Here are three of my favorite meals that are great to freeze and reheat:

Beef Stew

1 tablespoon oil
1 32-ounce package stew beef, or 2 pounds round roast,
  cut into chunks
1 cup water
1 onion, sliced
2 cloves garlic, minced
Spices (bay leaves, allspice, salt, pepper) to taste
Raw vegetables (carrots, celery, potatoes) cut into bite-sized pieces
Canned vegetables (corn, peas)
2 tablespoons cornstarch, dissolved in water

Put oil in large pot. Brown stew beef or round roast. Add water, onion, garlic and your favorite spices. Simmer one hour.

Add any of your favorite raw vegetables. Continue to simmer for one-half hour. If you'd like to add canned vegetables, drain them first, then simmer for the last ten minutes. Just before serving, dissolve two tablespoons of cornstarch in water, stir until smooth, then stir into stew.

Vegetarian Chili

1 tablespoon oil
1 pound all-vegetable burger crumbles
1 onion, diced
1½ tablespoons chili powder
14 ounces ketchup
1 cup water
1 12-ounce can light red kidney beans, drained

Put oil in large pot. Brown crumbles together with onion. Stir in chili powder, ketchup, water and light red kidney beans. Simmer for one hour.

Spicy Chicken Chili

1 tablespoon oil
1 onion, sliced
2 cloves garlic
1 pound cooked chicken, cubed
2 12-ounce cans Great Northern beans, drained
8 ounces green chilies, chopped

1 teaspoon oregano
½ teaspoon cumin
½ teaspoon salt
1 cup uncooked macaroni

Put oil in large pot. Sauté onion and garlic. Add cooked chicken. Add Great Northern beans and chopped green chilies. Stir in oregano, cumin, salt and uncooked macaroni. Bring to a boil, then reduce heat to a simmer for one hour.

You must remember to thaw the meal in advance, of course. Each night after dinner, stop and ask yourself, "What will we have for dinner tomorrow?" If you need to thaw something, move it from the freezer to the refrigerator. The next day, simply heat, and dinner's ready.

Freezers operate most efficiently when they are full. Until you have the time to fill yours with food, fill it with various-size containers of water. Once frozen, these containers will do a great job of keeping food and drinks cold for your next picnic. Buying bags of ice will be a thing of the past.

Clipping Coupons

If you follow the advice already given, you may never use a coupon again! They're only available for brand-name items, which you probably will no longer be purchasing.

Today, most of the biggest grocery chains double coupons, with a maximum of one dollar off an item. Even so, you can usually still get an off-brand for less, so I rarely take advantage of this double-coupon offer. But every once in a while, grocers will double coupons to a maximum of two dollars. Here's when coupons can really pay off, especially when the item you want to buy is also on sale. These are the times when you should stock up, even if it means storing the items under your bed or in your coat closet!

Preparing Lunches for School

The average elementary school lunch costs about $2. If you have two children buying lunch every day, you're spending $724 a year on their lunches ($2 × two lunches = $4 × 181 school days = $724). Unfortunately, I can almost guarantee that up to half of what your child buys is being thrown away every day. As a once-a-month volunteer in our school cafeteria, I see all those trays of barely eaten fish sticks, corn dogs and stale peanut-butter-and-jelly sandwiches being stacked at the dishwashing window as the kids run out to the playground.

If you packed their lunch instead you could do the following:

- *Save more than $500 a year if you have two kids.* If you stay away from the prepackaged snacks and meals, you can easily put together a nutritious lunch for about a quarter, plus thirty-five cents for a carton of milk.

- *Pack foods they like, in the quantity you know they'll eat, and nothing will be wasted.* Maybe your child loves corn dogs, so you know he'll eat the school lunch on corn dog day. He may eat the corn dog, but what about the mixed vegetables and canned peaches that come with it? Is he eating that too? If you packed his lunch instead, you could give him the portion you know he'll eat. My daughter will eat only half of a peanut-butter-and-jelly sandwich and half of a canned pear every day, so those are exactly the portions she receives.

Using what my daughter will eat as an example, here's a comparison of school lunches (on left) versus lunches packed at home (on right):

School	Lunches Packed at Home
Stale peanut-butter-and-jelly sandwich (At least half gets thrown away.)	Half of fresh peanut-butter-and-jelly sandwich in a plastic sandwich bag that has been used all week*
Two slices of canned peaches (All gets thrown away, as she dislikes peaches.)	Half of a canned pear packed in a reusable thermos, or small piece of fresh fruit
Mixed vegetables, room temperature (Even I wouldn't eat this!)	Two carrot sticks wrapped in a piece of plastic wrap (She doesn't really love carrot sticks, but if I insist she get a vegetable, this is what she prefers.)
Sugar cookie with sprinkles (No problem here!)	Two homemade oatmeal cookies (more nutritious than sugar cookie)
Carton of milk	Carton of milk
Total cost for 181 days of school: $362.00 per child	**Total cost for 181 days of school: $108.60 per child**

---

* Reusing plastic sandwich bags won't make a significant dent in the family budget. But recycling just makes good sense. You don't throw away your Tupperware, do you?

Packing lunches will not save you money if you stuff them with pudding snacks, Lunchables, juice boxes and prepackaged applesauce. If you want to include Jell-O, applesauce or potato chips, buy them in bulk, and package them yourself.

Here are a few good ideas for children's school lunches:

- *Pack their favorite dry cereal in a thermos.* Add a piece of fruit, celery with peanut butter and milk to pour over the cereal.
- *Imitate their classmate's Lunchables for a fraction of the cost.* Cut a piece of lunch meat and a piece of cheese into quarters. Add four crackers or a piece of bread, a piece of fruit, two oatmeal cookies and milk.
- *Spread a tortilla with cream cheese or mayonnaise; add a slice of turkey and shredded carrots or lettuce.* Roll it tight, and seal it in plastic wrap. Add a piece of fruit, homemade granola bar or loose granola in a bag and milk.
- *Put peanut butter and bananas in pita bread.* Add carrot sticks, popcorn and milk.

When packing lunches, try to keep from sending the same lunch every day. With some variety, your children will learn to expand their tastes. Make it easy on yourself by using leftovers. Pasta salad, meatloaf sandwiches, leftover pizza and that last handful of popcorn can all be included in a packed lunch.

Preparing Work Lunches

Going out to lunch with coworkers can make a significant dent in the wallet. At an average cost of $6 a day, such lunches can amount to more than $1,500 in a year's time. Bring your lunch to work instead, and you'll save time, money and calories. There will be no more standing in line with the noon-hour crowd waiting to order or waiting for a table.

Packing lunch the night before, using leftovers from earlier in the week, can be done quickly, especially if you're packing your children's lunches at the same time. Encourage your coworkers to pack their lunches, too. You'll have more time to enjoy each other's company. Eager to leave the building? A short walk after lunch is a great stress reliever before returning to an afternoon of work.

Eating Out

If you eat out on a regular basis, I recommend you total all your restaurant bills, including tips, for a month (see Chapter 9). You'll be shocked at how much money you're spending. Consider how much time you're spending driving to and from the restaurant and waiting for your meal, time you could be at home instead.

I am not suggesting you never take the family out for a meal again. But I think you will be surprised at the amount of money you're spending. Let's say you come up with an honest monthly total of $400. That's a conservative estimate for most families of four. Some spend well over $700 a month. Multiply the amount you spend each month by twelve. Now you have a good idea of how much you're spending each year by eating out.

Now, let's assume you can satisfy your family with similarly delicious (and in most cases healthier) food for 10 percent of the cost. The difference in a year's time is $4,300 to $7,500. How many hours do you have to work to earn that amount of money (after taxes)? Is it worth it?

Here's one more reason to eat out less often. A Tufts University research study found that the more often people of all ages ate in restaurants, the more body fat they had. What's more, they consumed more calories and fat, but less fiber.

Eating out can be convenient, and it can be fun. But it is also very expensive, not to mention time-consuming. Would you forgo the habit of eating out if it meant you could work fewer hours and spend more time with your family?

Getting Used to Leftovers

If you shudder at the thought of eating a leftover, yet you are eager to lead a simpler life, I recommend you get accustomed to meals made from leftovers. The amount of time and money you save by eating leftovers is worth whatever it is that bothers you. It may help you to know that many of the meals served in restaurants consist of ingredients left over from the day before.

Gardening

Do your children think vegetables come from the grocery store? Show them the glorious wonders of our Earth, and how to put a little love back into it, by starting your own vegetable garden. It's a wonderful family activity, and you may even save a bit of money, too. Besides, there's something special about picking tomatoes or snipping basil from your garden for dinner that same evening.

Several years ago I started a small four-by-five-foot vegetable garden in our side yard. The kids and I planted eight tomato plants and some pumpkin seeds. The tomatoes grew splendidly. The pumpkins did not. The next year we tried tomatoes, pumpkins and green beans. The tomatoes grew splendidly. The pumpkins did not. And we collected a total of five bean pods. Last year we switched to tomatoes and basil. Complete success! This year we'll be doubling the size of the garden and trying two other vegetables in addition to tomatoes and basil.

In spite of the failures, our garden has provided us an abundance of riches. We've grown tomatoes so sweet our pasta never tasted so good, and more fresh basil than the biggest pesto lover could ever eat. We've reveled in the glory of our tomato plants that grow inches literally overnight. We've marveled as our tomatoes went from white to yellow to pale green to bright green to soft orange and eventually to a rich, deep, juicy red. And we've shaken our fists at the critters who managed to taste our produce before we could. See how much one tiny garden can do for a family? Imagine what you can experience with a little more space and know-how.

If you've never planted a vegetable garden, here are simple instructions:

- *Find a level patch of ground, preferably away from trees and shrubs, that gets at least six hours of full sun each day.* Make sure your garden hose can reach the area you choose. Clear the spot of debris like sticks, rocks and grass.
- *When the soil is moist (not too wet or too dry), dig down eight to twelve inches, turning the soil until it is nice and loose.* Be patient. This

takes time and energy. If you find worms, rejoice. That means your soil is healthy. If not, add topsoil, manure or compost to improve the soil quality.

- *If your soil doesn't have good drainage (water sits instead of soaks), prepare a raised garden bed instead.* Using brick or lumber that is eight inches high, outline your garden. Fill the plot with topsoil or healthy soil from other areas of your yard.

- *Plan to grow vegetables and herbs your family will enjoy eating.* I recommend tomatoes, basil, parsley, summer squash and green beans, because they are easy to grow and don't take up a lot of space. Vegetables are designated as "warm season" or "cool season," depending on the weather they need for optimum growing. Warm-season vegetables require warm soil and high temperatures. They are killed by frost so cannot be planted until after your area's final frost. They include beans, cucumber, eggplants, peppers, squash, tomatoes and such herbs as basil and parsley. Cool-season vegetables can tolerate colder soil. They can be planted in very early spring to harvest in early summer or can be planted in late summer for harvest in the fall. They include beets, broccoli, cabbage, carrots, lettuce, peas, spinach and onions.

- *Be sure to select vegetables that your garden space will accommodate.*

- *If you want to grow your vegetables from seeds, check the seed packets to determine the best planting time.* A bulb will significantly speed growing time. Get the kids involved. They'll be fascinated to watch some plants shoot up practically overnight. Otherwise, purchase starter plants at a garden store.

Here's a simple layout for a four-by-five-foot garden:

Tomatoes	
Basil	Parsley
Carrots	Onions
Green Beans	

Here are a few additional tips:

- *Install a low, sturdy fence* (chicken wire is fine) around your garden to keep pests out.
- *Don't hesitate to ask for advice from successful gardeners.* They hang out at gardening stores. They already know what grows best in your climate and will advise you on the best time to plant.
- *Be prepared to stake vegetables that grow tall to prevent them from falling over and breaking at the stem.* A sturdy dowel (one per plant) and loosely tied string will do the job.
- *If you can't find a good spot in your yard for a garden, try planting in containers that sit in a sunny location on your deck or porch.* I put a tiny basil plant in a flower pot on my deck, which eventually grew to the size of a small bush.
- *Don't forget to water appropriately.* If you'll be taking a vacation, ask a neighbor to help out.

Can't possibly find the time or desire to plant a garden? Then set aside a morning to visit an orchard to pick fruit with your kids. Use the fruit to make pie or jelly. Eating food that you've grown or gathered is extremely satisfying.

Composting

One of the best ways to ensure a successful garden is to provide it with good soil. By composting, you can turn yard and kitchen waste into a rich mix of soil ideal for any garden. Ask anyone who composts. It's simple and nearly impossible to do incorrectly. It costs nothing. It returns waste to the Earth instead of the landfill. It contributes to a healthier garden.

Composting is so easy, you can put the kids in charge of it and teach them a good lesson at the same time. Here's how it's done.

1. Find a nice level spot in your yard (on soil, not concrete) about three-by-six feet. Leave enough room so you can move all the way around the spot. Sun or shade is acceptable. Tucked away in a corner, behind a tree or shed, is perfectly acceptable.

2. Enclose the area with mesh, chicken wire, brick, or any material that will help keep your compost in one place. The sides should be no more than waist high, as you'll need to be able to turn your pile every now and then. You might want to leave one side completely open for easier access, but if you have small children or a dog, it may be best to enclose all sides.

3. Keep a container in your kitchen to collect food wastes. It should hold about two gallons and have a lid. Store under the sink or on your countertop. Periodically empty the container, as well as yard waste (see list on page 44) onto one half of your compost area. Leave the other half empty. Every six weeks or so (more often in the summer, less often in winter), use a spade or pitchfork to turn the pile. If the pile starts to

smell, turn it more often. Turning your pile is the only requirement for successful composting. It causes three important things to occur: (1) it mixes the wet stuff with the dry stuff; (2) it combines partially composted material with new material; and (3) it adds oxygen to the pile, which reenergizes the organisms that are doing the work.

4. After a few months, abandon your pile and begin a new one in the empty half of your space. Continue to turn your original pile every six weeks or so until it looks rich and brown and ready to be added to your garden. (If it appears to be ready, but it's the wrong time of year for gardening, don't worry. Like people, compost only improves with age!)

Composting is so easy, there's not much that could go wrong. But here are a few tips:

- *If the pile seems dry, water it with a garden hose.* You'll need to stick the hose into the sides of the pile to make sure it gets good and wet.
- *If the pile seems too wet from too much rain, lay a tarp over it until the rain stops.* Then spread the pile around a bit to help it dry out.
- *If the pile smells bad, turn it more frequently and cut back on the amount of grass clippings.*

At the end of this chapter I've listed a couple of good books about composting that should address any concerns that might arise. They also describe how you can compost in a container if you don't have the yard space.

Once you become an experienced composter, you'll easily determine what can and cannot be added to your pile. In the meantime, refer to the list here. And remember these three rules:

(1) if it isn't biodegradable, it isn't compostable; (2) the greater the variety, the better; and (3) cutting big items into small pieces will speed the process.

What a wonderful, wholesome experience for you and your family: you create compost to nourish the soil. Your rich soil produces vegetables grown in your own garden to nourish your body. Your garden waste is returned to the compost pile where it will eventually nourish the soil once again.

Include these materials:

Ashes (wood, not coal)

Coffee grounds (including the filter)

Eggshells (crushed)

Flowers

Fruit, fruit peels and cores

Grass clippings

Human hair (unless chemically treated)

Leaves (best if ground by your lawn mower)

Manure (chicken, cow, horse)

Peanut shells

Pine needles

Plant trimmings

Sawdust (from untreated lumber)

Tea leaves

Vegetables, vegetable peels and stalks

Avoid these materials:

Bones

Coal

Charcoal

Diseased plants

Feces (pet and human)

Fish

Grease

Kitchen oils and fats

Meat

Preserving Food

Preserving the food you've picked or grown is a wonderful way to enjoy your harvest year-round. It doesn't take much time and, like gardening, is a wonderful family activity. It also is a simple way to share the fruits of your labor with others for gift-giving occasions.

Whether you gather food from a farmer's market, an orchard, or your own backyard garden, it is best to begin the preservation process as soon as possible after gathering. Your family will love the fresh taste of food preserved soon after harvest over commercially prepared food. And you will like knowing that food preserved soon after harvesting retains significantly more nutrients and vitamins than foods purchased at the grocer.

Preserve your harvest by freezing it or by home canning. Here's how.

Freezing

- *Raw vegetables.* Wash raw vegetables, and cut them into bite-size pieces. Steam vegetables, then cool quickly by plunging them into ice water. Blot dry, then immediately freeze in zip-style bags. Be sure to label and date each bag.
- *Tomatoes.* Freeze your tomato harvest by first dunking whole, cored tomatoes in boiling water for one minute. Doing so will make the skin easily peel off. Freeze whole or in slices in zip-style bags. Or prepare your favorite tomato-based recipes before freezing.
- *Fruit.* The ideal method for freezing fruit is also the simplest. Carefully wash the fruit and place individually on baking

sheets. Place sheets in the freezer. Once frozen, immediately place fruit in zip-style bags or containers. Date and label containers, and return to the freezer. Or you can freeze fruit in water, juice or light syrup (½ cup sugar and 4 cups water heated until sugar dissolves). Place clean, raw fruit in a container, then add chilled liquid, leaving up to an inch of headspace to allow the liquid to expand.

- *Herbs.* You've probably discovered that herbs can be terribly expensive and less flavorful during the winter months. Savor your bountiful herb harvest by taking the following simple steps: Cut six-inch stalks, and gently brush away soil. Freeze on baking sheet, then transfer to zip-style bags, removing any air before sealing. Label and freeze the bags. Basil will discolor in the freezer unless blanched. To prepare basil for freezing, use tongs to quickly dip stalks and leaves in boiling water, then dry on towels. Once dry, store the basil in zip-style bags, removing any air before sealing. Label and freeze the bags.

- *Herb sauces and spreads.* If you love the taste of fresh pesto or other herb sauces and spreads, make as much of the recipe as your herb harvest allows. Spoon the sauce or spread into ice cube trays. Once frozen, transfer cubes to zip-style bags. Label and freeze the bags. Come mid-January, you'll be glad you did!

How Long in the Freezer?

Your foods will retain their best flavor if left in the freezer no longer than the time indicated here. Food stored beyond recommended time will still be safe to eat, but flavor, texture and nutritional value may be affected:

Fruit (citrus): 4–6 months

Fruit (non-citrus): 8–12 months

Herbs (raw or blanched): 6 months

Herb sauces/spreads: 6 months

Vegetables (raw, blanched): 8–12 months

Vegetables (cooked): 8–12 months

Canning

Preserving food by canning dates back to the early 1800s, when food was first preserved in widemouthed jars sealed with cork. Later, tin canisters ("cans") were considered a better container for preserved food. Although not long afterward the glass jar with threaded tips was invented and is still in use today, the term canning is still in use.

The theory of preserving food by canning is simple: Airtight containers (jars) are filled with food and sealed. Very high heat is applied to the filled containers, destroying bacteria and creating a vacuum to prevent any further bacterial growth.

The materials needed to preserve food by canning depend on the amount of acid in the food to be preserved.

High-acid foods require less heat to kill bacteria. These foods can be preserved by a simple "water-bath" method, which requires the following materials:

- Mason jars and the two-piece, rubber-edged lids designed for these jars

High-Acid Foods	Low-Acid Foods
Chutneys	Asparagus
Condiments	Beans (green, lima, snap and wax)
Fruits	Brussels sprouts
Fruit juices	Carrots
Jams	Corn
Jellies	Cucumber
Fruit spreads	Mushrooms
Pickles	Peas
Relishes	Peppers
Sauces	Potatoes (new white and sweet)
Sauerkraut	Pumpkin
Vinegars	Squash
Tomatoes (can be treated as high acid by adding two tablespoons of bottled lemon juice per quart of tomatoes)	

- A pot with a lid, large enough to allow four inches of space above a jar once it is set inside the pot
- A wire rack to hold jars away from the direct heat at the bottom of the pot
- A jar lifter or tongs large enough to lift a heavy, sealed jar

To safely kill the bacteria in low-acid foods, replace the pot and wire rack previously listed with a pressure canner. This canner, equipped with a gauge and petcock, is designed to apply sufficient heat (240 degrees Fahrenheit) to destroy deadly bacteria that can more easily grow in low-acid foods. The amount of pressure and processing time depends on the food being preserved and the altitude of your home.

The process of preserving foods is as follows:

1. Sterilize jars in boiling water for ten minutes.

2. For high-acid foods, clean, peel and slice foods into bite-size pieces. Pack one jar at a time with food, then add hot liquid, allowing sufficient headspace. Gently press the food with a rubber spatula to release trapped air. Apply the clean lid, and secure with a clean screw-ring. Place jars on rack in pot of hot water, making sure the water level is at least one inch above the jar. The jars should not touch each other. Bring the water to a full boil, then put the lid on the pot, and set the timer for the number of minutes specified in your recipe. Reduce heat to a gentle boil, and add more hot water when necessary to maintain water level.

   For low-acid foods, cut food to appropriate sizes, then place in a pan, cover with water, and bring to boil. Reduce heat and simmer for three minutes. Pack the food loosely in warm jars, one at a time, and then add boiling water, allowing about one-half inch headspace. Gently press the food with a rubber spatula to release trapped air. Apply the clean lid, and secure with a clean screw-ring. Place each jar in rack provided with pressure canner. Follow directions that accompany your pressure canner for necessary amount of pressure and proper processing time.

3. When time is up, turn off heat and use tongs to remove hot jars to a flat surface protected with towels.

4. Once jars have completely cooled (twelve hours or more), carefully test the seals by pressing the center of the lid. If the lid does not move, the jar is properly sealed, and you will enjoy your harvest for up to a year or more. If a jar is not properly sealed, put it in the refrigerator and consume within the week.

5. Date each jar, and then store your canned food in a cool, dry, dark place.

You'll find proper canning equipment available for purchase through this website: www.homecanning.com.

To a simple family, purchasing, preparing and eating meals together are activities to be enjoyed, not endured. By implementing some, or all, of the ideas presented in this chapter, you'll discover food nourishes not only the body, but the soul as well.

Resources

For more detailed information on the ideas presented in this chapter, read these books:

America's All-Time Favorite Canning & Preserving Recipes (Better Homes and Gardens, 1996)

The Big Book of Preserving the Harvest by Carol W. Costenbader (Storey Publishing, 1997)

Brown Bag Success: Making Healthy Lunches Your Kids Won't Trade by Sandra K. Nissenberg and Barbara N. Pearl (Chronimed Publishing, 1997)

Composting by Liz Ball (Workman Publishing Company, 1998)

Fast, Easy Vegetable Garden by Jerry Baker (Plume, 1999)

The Frugal Gardener: How to Have More Garden for Less Money by Catriona Tudor Erler (Rodale, 1999)

Let It Rot! The Gardener's Guide to Composting by Stu Campbell (Storey Books, 1998)

Once-a-Month Cooking: A Proven System for Spending Less Time in the Kitchen and Enjoying Delicious, Homemade Meals Every Day by Mimi Wilson and Mary Beth Lagerborg (St. Martin's Griffin, 1999)

The Allens—A Simpler Family

Jeannie and Don Allen have three children. Until seven years ago, the family was well supported by two full-time incomes. But once their second child, now age 6, was born, Jeannie yearned for a simpler life for her family. To her, that meant quitting her job. She didn't expect it would be easy to live without her $900-a-month salary, but once she did her homework Jeannie realized it might not be as difficult as she feared. "The cost of after-school care for my oldest child; my meals, snacks and beverages at work; gasoline; and taxes didn't leave me much to take home," she found. If they could scale back on just a few things, Jeannie figured they could get by on (husband's) then $35,000 annual salary. She was right.

After Jeannie quit her job, the couple made "getting out of debt" a priority. With help from their local Consumer Credit Counseling Service, they eliminated $3,000 in credit card debt within two years. "We now have an American Express card to use for emergencies only," she said.

Jeannie has used her time at home to find other ways to reduce this family of five's living expenses. Their grocery bill, once $500 per month, is now $350 per month. "I only buy meats when they are on sale and refuse to pay more than $1.99 a pound for any meat. I'm not brand loyal, and have found the store-brand is just as good as the name-brand in most instances." Jeannie uses coupons only if the item is already on sale, thus making it a worthwhile purchase. And she never shops without a list—and she firmly sticks to it. Don has grown accustomed to taking leftovers to work for lunch most days, and only goes out to lunch with co-workers once a week.

Although being a full-time stay-at-home mother can be stressful at times, Jeannie believes the lives of all family members have improved since she quit her job. "I'm not rushing to get dinner on the table after being at work all day. We eat a home-cooked dinner every night unless we *choose* to make it a take-out night. We have the time to sit at the table and talk each evening. And my house is clean!" she reports. Jeannie has also found that her youngest children, who have never been in child care, are sick less often than her oldest was at their age.

With their scaled-back lifestyle, the Allens celebrate a simpler Christmas that doesn't leave them mired in debt for months afterwards. "We don't over-emphasize the gift giving and receiving aspect of the holiday, so our children don't expect a huge bonanza of presents on Christmas morning. Instead, we set a specific dollar amount for each child, and stick to it." Jeannie begins shopping for the holiday in August, watching for sales, and sticks to the family policy of paying for purchases with cash only.

This simpler family of five is happy to now own a 1,500 square foot home in Louisiana—"well, the bank owns it, but we are paying on it!" Jeannie laughs. Until recently, the Allens were a one-car family. But as the children got older and sports schedules began to conflict, a second vehicle became a necessity. So they searched for a bargain and found a 1984 Volkswagen Rabbit in great condition. "With a diesel engine, it gets a phenomenal 42 miles to the gallon, on fuel that is much cheaper than unleaded!" Jeannie reports.

CHAPTER 3

Clothes

*"Happiness is inward, and not outward; and so,
it does not depend on what we have, but on what
we are."*

—Henry Van Dyke

DESPITE ALL THE HYPE and marketing dollars spent by clothing manufacturers to convince us otherwise, the purpose of clothing is to protect our body from the elements. It should keep us warm in winter, cool in summer, and dry when the weather is wet. And if the quality is superior, our clothing can serve us well for years, so we don't need to buy more clothes every season.

Most families spend 10 to 15 percent of the family budget on clothing. That means a family with a combined net income of

$50,000 spends $5,000 to $7,500 each year for clothing alone. The ideas in this chapter encourage you to take a simpler, more practical approach to clothing yourself and your family. Implement these ideas, and your total family clothing budget will be smaller. And all the time previously spent shopping for clothes can be spent on more meaningful family activities instead.

Find Your Style

There's a certain style of clothing that is best suited to each body type. And not every color looks good on every person. To simplify your clothing, determine the style that best suits your body and the colors that best suit your coloring. Your spouse and your children should do the same. Stick with those basics. Keep it simple.

If you look best in black, buy several nice pairs of black pants, or black skirts, in a style to suit your body type. If you don't already own them, get a sturdy pair of black shoes. Then purchase several nice sport shirts, button-down shirts or blouses in colors that complement you. Now you have a basic dress-up wardrobe for work or other occasions when jeans won't suffice. Use colorful scarves or ties to add variety to your basic wardrobe.

Purge your closet of all the extra clothing you don't need or wear. Take extras to a consignment store (see instructions later in this chapter), or donate them to charity.

Developing and sticking to a basic wardrobe will help to simplify your life. Shopping for clothing will be quick and easy. Because you've determined the colors and the style that work best for you, you can quickly zero in on what you need. You'll save money, as you will be purchasing only what you need, instead of every new fashion to hit the stores. You'll have plenty of extra closet space as you get rid of everything that doesn't suit your basic needs.

Simplifying your family's wardrobe is the perfect example of how less is more:

Less	More
Less clothes in your closet and drawers	More space for other items that currently clutter your bedroom
Less time spent shopping for clothes	More time spent with family
Less money spent on unnecessary clothes	More money to spend on essentials

Of course, you'll still find yourself in need of more clothing from time to time. When a clothing need arises, remember to jot it in your Needs Notebook, as described in Chapter 1. As you shop for these clothes, don't pay full retail price, ever. Wait until a store is stocked with next season's fashions, then go and buy last season's fashions at steep discounts. Early January is an especially good time to shop. This is when retailers need to unload any clothing not sold over the holidays.

For much better prices on clothing for your family, consider the ideas presented in the rest of this chapter.

Shop at Outlet Stores

Outlet malls are springing up in nearly every city. According to *Value Retail News*, the number of outlet retailers has more than tripled over the past twelve years. Nearly every major interstate is graced with at least a few. In between each mall are dozens of billboards begging travelers to stop and take advantage of the bargains. But how can we really be sure the prices at these stores are less than at any other store? There's only one way—compare the prices. Before you make the trip to your nearest outlet mall, determine how much the department store in your area is charging for the items you want to purchase. Compare these prices with those at the outlet store. Be sure to compare quality too.

Some manufacturers and distributors open a clearance center adjacent to their plant in order to sell damaged merchandise. Typically, these stores look like warehouses, with cement floors and clothing strewn all over the place, instead of like the beautifully designed interiors of stores in the outlet malls.

Whether the outlet store you shop in is part of an outlet mall or adjacent to the plant where the clothes are manufactured, do your homework. Be certain the prices really are bargains. And shop only for what you need.

Purchase Clothing Secondhand

If you've never purchased secondhand clothing, you'll be thrilled to learn how much time and money it can save you. Before you prepare to buy another piece of brand-new clothing, consider these reasons for purchasing secondhand instead:

- *Price.* Instead of paying thirty-five dollars for Gap pants and T-shirts, you'll pay four dollars.

- *Value.* Designer clothes are nice to own, but not so nice to pay for. If you purchase secondhand, you'll get great value for your money.
- *Lack of risk.* When you pay a dollar for a pair of children's pants, the inevitable torn knees and grass stains are less bothersome. When you pay fifty cents for a pair of Reeboks, you won't panic when they get caked with mud on day one.
- *Shrinkage.* The previous owner has already taken care of any shrinkage that may occur.
- *Charity.* Because many secondhand stores are operated to raise funds for schools or charities, your purchase is helping to support a good cause.
- *Comfort.* Having already been washed numerous times, secondhand clothing is typically softer and more comfortable, a feature your kids will especially like.
- *Recycling.* Promoting reusing and recycling is a valuable lesson for the family to live by.

Here are your best sources for secondhand clothing:

Consignment Stores

Consignment stores sell secondhand merchandise for the purpose of making a profit. Store owners get their merchandise from individuals who get a percentage of the profit (often 50 percent) after the sale.

The prices in consignment stores are usually lower than outlet stores but higher than the prices in thrift stores, where the clothing is donated. Store owners are selective about the quality of what they will sell, so you can expect to find nice, clean clothing that is free of stains or tears while shopping there.

Because they need to move merchandise quickly to make room for more, many stores use color-coded tags to reflect additional savings. Look for a sign when you enter the store. You may find that all clothing with a yellow tag is 75 percent off, a blue tag is 50 percent off, and an orange tag is 25 percent off.

Here are the major advantages to shopping consignment stores:

- *Prices are significantly better than retail.*
- *Quality is very good.* Because the store manager determines which clothing is suitable for her store, you benefit from her prescreening. If you like what you see in a particular store, you can probably count on it to be a reliable source for good clothing.
- *Clothing is displayed in a sensible fashion.* Typically, you'll find clothing arranged by size, type, and sometimes by color. Unlike department stores, you'll find all pairs of size-ten pants are displayed together, making it easy to find something you like.
- *Service is excellent.* These small business owners are usually wonderful at helping you find what you need and may be willing to phone you if an item you want comes in.

Selling to a Consignment Shop

Consignment stores offer an opportunity for you to get cash for the clothing your family no longer needs, provided it is in good condition. Here are some tips for selling your clothing in this manner:

- Separate your family's clothing by season, as some stores are interested only in next-season merchandise
- Clean all clothing, paying special attention to stains that could cause a clothing item to be rejected.

   Here's a homemade stain remover that works wonders on some of the toughest stains, including infant spit-ups: ½ cup of dishwasher detergent (like Cascade), ½ cup of powdered stain remover (like Biz or Clorox II) and 2 gallons of hot water. Soak clothes overnight.
- Check the yellow pages for all consignment stores in your area. Ask whether they charge a "consignor's fee" and the amount of the fee. Find out how often consignees are paid. Ask how long clothes are kept (sixty days is standard). Find out what the owner does with unsold merchandise (she may invite you to pick up anything not sold or ask that you agree to allow her to donate your unsold items).

Thrift Stores

You'll find some of the best prices on used clothing at thrift shops. These stores, including Goodwill and Salvation Army, sell clothing and other household items that individuals have donated, as well as merchandise obtained through special arrangement with retail stores or manufacturers. For this reason, it is not uncommon to find store tags still hanging on some clothing.

   Thrift stores are usually operated by charitable organizations or schools that rely on the income the store generates to fund their causes. Because they pay nothing for the items they sell, they are able to charge less than consignment stores.

Some people think shopping thrift stores should be reserved for people who are desperately poor. They mistakenly believe that if you have enough money, you should not shop thrift stores because you are taking merchandise away from people who need it most. The truth is, thrift store operators are eager for everyone to shop their stores. The profits they make from your purchases fund the causes they support. In fact, in some places thrift stores are being built in upscale neighborhoods. The store operators are simply trying to increase earnings by enticing shoppers who have more money to spend.

Here are the major advantages to shopping thrift stores:

- *Selection.* Some thrift stores are enormous. It would not be uncommon to find 100 pairs of size-ten jeans on the rack.
- *Price.* Because items have been donated, the prices in thrift stores are excellent.
- *Variety.* Because of the sheer volume of donations, selections change daily. And through special arrangements with area retailers or manufacturers, you may find some brand-new clothing.
- *Inclusiveness.* At large thrift stores, you'll find not only adult and children's clothing, but secondhand toys, shoes, purses, hats, scarves and other accessories as well.
- *Uniqueness.* Full-price retail stores tend to have a limited number of clothing styles each season. Thrift stores, on the other hand, sell styles popular over recent years.

Yard Sales

Yard sales have the very best prices on secondhand clothing, particularly for children's clothes. The primary reason most people have a yard sale is not to make lots of money, but to get rid of all the stuff they no longer want. The result is great merchandise at great prices. These savings can mean a lot—the difference between the income from a full-time and part-time job for many families.

Bring along your Needs Notebook (see Chapter 1) when shopping yard sales. Don't shop just for items you need immediately. Purchasing in advance is essential to reducing your expenses. If you see a pair of snow boots or a nice fleece jacket for a good price, grab it, even if the temperature is hovering in the nineties. Come December, you'll be glad you did.

The next time you shop a yard sale for clothing, follow this advice from veteran yard sale shopper Alicia Collins:

- Newspapers advertise sales beginning on Thursdays. Look for sales in upscale neighborhoods, and map out the sales you intend to visit.
- Arrive fifteen to twenty minutes before the advertised start of the sale to get the best selection.
- The best prices and selection are on children's clothing.
- If you are interested in something that is stained or torn, offer a discounted price.
- If you are buying more than one item, offer a single price for everything ("I'll take all of this for five dollars."). The seller is usually happy to oblige. They don't want to move it back inside at the end of the day.

While shopping yard sales for clothing, look at the bedding items too. I've gotten wonderful thick, warm blankets that match my kids' bedrooms for practically nothing. And if the price is right, it's always a good idea to buy a few extra sheets, spreads and blankets. They're ideal for picnics, outdoor concerts, back-yard tents and bedroom forts.

Secondhand Shopping Advice

Here are some things to keep in mind before purchasing second-hand clothes:

- The clothing is not returnable, so check each piece closely for missing buttons, tears and stains. (Leave the item behind unless you can easily make repairs.)
- Many of these stores don't have dressing rooms, so if you have never been able to fit into a size-eight pair of slacks, don't buy size-eight slacks, even if they do look a little bit larger than usual.
- It can be tempting to buy more than you need when the prices are this good. Don't clutter the closets with more cloth-ing than you can possibly wear.
- Buy good-quality items that are currently too large for your children if you are confident they'll wear the items down the road.
- Don't buy anything that isn't comfortable, no matter how good the price. You aren't likely to wear it more than once if it doesn't feel good.
- Be sure to bring along your Needs Notebook (Chapter 1). That way you won't miss out on a bargain because you forgot you needed it or couldn't remember your daughter's size.
- Do you already own a great outfit but need to replace the but-tons? There's nothing wrong with buying something just for the buttons if the price is good. New buttons can be expensive.

- If you have a child who loves to play dress-up, you will find secondhand shops a virtual gold mine of treasures.

Take Advantage of Hand-Me-Downs

Children seem to outgrow clothing faster than they wear it out. You could spend a fortune every few months keeping up with their clothing needs, or you could save the money and arrange to swap clothing with family and friends instead. This idea makes perfect sense, not so much because you need the donation, but because, like recycling paper, plastic and aluminum cans, recycling clothing is kind to the environment. It teaches a good lesson to your children—and it brings you one step closer to being a simpler family.

My friend Kathleen, the mother of twins, participates in a well-organized exchange twice each year. Arranged by her area's Mothers of Twins Club, the event gives parents of twins the opportunity to obtain clothing, toys and other items for their twins as well as sell items they no longer need. Although not free, everything is very inexpensive and has been a huge help in offsetting the cost of twins.

If you are unable to arrange an exchange group, put out the word to family and friends that you'll be happy to accept any clothing they no longer want. You won't sound like a charity case. Just say that you would be happy to take any hand-me-downs they no longer need. You'll probably find most people are happy to know someone else will get good use of their items. Be sure to exchange the favor by passing along the clothes you and your kids outgrow, as well as their toys and bikes.

My dear neighbor Sue has been a great source of used clothing for my kids, and sometimes for me too. Every couple of months she goes through a cleaning spurt and calls me to say she has a few bags for me. Because Sue's daughter is nine years older than my daughter, and her son is seven years older than my son, the clothes she gives me never fit right away. But I don't turn them down, because they *will* fit in a few years. The work it takes to sort and store hand-me-downs is well worth it. Just last week, my son ruined one of his last few pairs of long pants. I ran down to the basement, sorted through the "long pants" boxes, and found four pairs that fit perfectly.

Here is my advice for sorting all hand-me-downs and clothing you've purchased for the future. When the time comes for your children to wear the items you've collected, they will surely find something they refuse to wear. Avoid taking up space with these unwanted items by immediately donating them to your favorite charity.

A Simple Storage Solution

As you collect hand-me-downs and other clothing you purchased but don't immediately need (like snow boots or too-large pants), you will need a practical storage system until your children grow into them. Use sturdy boxes of uniform shape (boxes that hold paper are ideal and may be free for the asking at office supply stores). If dampness is a potential problem, purchase large plastic tubs with lids, especially cheap just after the holidays.

Large families may find it best to sort the clothing by sex and age of child (boy 6–7, girl 6–7, boy 8–9, etc.). Smaller families can sort by type of clothing, mixing items for girls and boys in the same box. I have boxes labeled as follows:

Long Pants
Shorts
Short-Sleeve Shirts
Long-Sleeve Shirts
Sweatshirts/Sweaters
Coats/Jackets
Shoes/Boots

Mark each box or container clearly with the contents inside. Before a new season begins, pull out all appropriate boxes and plan a fitting session with your kids. With any luck, you will be able to assemble an entire season's wardrobe without a trip to the store.

Sew Your Own

Owning a basic sewing machine, even if just for straight stitches, can be a real money saver. If you don't own one, borrow one from a family member or add one to your Wish List (see Chapter 6).

A simple machine is all you will need. If you buy one new, you might find a free instruction class comes with the purchase. Once you know how to correctly thread the machine and adjust the tension, sewing straight seams will be easy, and you can do a lot once you learn the basics.

- Repair the hems or seams on clothing.

- Make simple repairs to dozens of household items, including blankets, towels, stuffed animals, backpacks and pockets in coats and pants.
- Shorten the length of pants, enabling you to take advantage of a bargain without spending more for a tailor.
- Turn children's pants into shorts when the knees get ruined.

You might also be pleased to discover that with a simple straight stitch you can make numerous household items and gifts like tablecloths, napkins, pillows (even ones with ruffled edges), curtains and valances.

But I *Need* an Abercrombie Shirt . . .

Teaching children to be savvy about prices and quality when they are young will benefit them throughout their life. If they have grown up wearing secondhand clothing, they already know that Mom and Dad aren't likely to cough up fifty dollars for a couple of designer T-shirts. They also have learned an important moral lesson. Through your gentle guidance you have shown them that designer clothes don't make them a better person and that the label on their shirt is not indicative of their own worth.

I'll never forget the day my daughter (then nine) and I were walking through the mall. As we neared an Abercrombie & Fitch store I challenged her to guess the price of a plain T-shirt displayed in the window. After careful consideration, she guessed five dollars. I could hardly contain my grin as I suggested we walk in and see if she was right. The look on her face was priceless (no pun intended) when she saw the twenty-six-dollar price tag.

But in spite of my best efforts, the day arrived, a year and a half later, when she wanted nothing else for Christmas but a shirt that said "Abercrombie" on the front. I bought one, and she was the happiest kid in the house on Christmas morning. But this definitely doesn't mean I'll be buying them on a regular (or even semiregular) basis. Most of the experts recommend the following, and my friends with older children agree:

- If your teenager wants a designer shirt and is willing to spend his own money to get it, give him your approval. It's his money to do with as he wishes.

- If you typically pay for his wardrobe, give your teenager the amount of money you'd be willing to spend on a shirt. If he insists on the designer shirt, he needs to come up with the difference.

- Remind your teenager, without nagging, that his friends should like him for who he is, not for the label on his shirt.

- Keep the television off as much as possible. Like it or not, the millions being spent by manufacturers on advertisements takes its toll on your children.

My friend Polly takes a different approach. When her daughters reached the age of being interested in clothes, she established a rule: Mom and Dad will never purchase a piece of clothing that advertises the name of a store. In addition to refusing to spend money on those particular items, Polly believes she is establishing a principle and an attitude that makes her children think. She lets them know that she doesn't think consumers should pay a company money for the privilege of advertising their product. Instead, she tries to point out to her children the many ways in which businesses exploit them.

A simple family lets its needs dictate its clothing and other purchases. If you truly want to maintain a simple, more meaningful family life, your clothes-buying habits should reflect that desire. By making smart choices about the way you spend your money, and by continuously working to scale back to a simpler way of life, you will be able to spend more time doing what is most important to you. Follow this advice, and you will not only teach your children important values, you will also save money that will enable you to spend more time at home.

CHAPTER 4

Household

"The darn trouble with cleaning the house is it gets dirty the next day anyway, so skip a week if you have to. The children are the most important thing."
—*Barbara Bush*

HOME IS THE biggest investment most families make both in terms of its monetary value and in terms of what happens within its walls. Home is the place where infants spend their first night in their very own crib, where toddlers take their first steps, where children fret over book reports and where teenagers agonize over love lives. It's where families gather for evening supper and extended families celebrate Thanksgiving dinners. Home is so important to us, we can easily spend more time and money than necessary to make it attractive and in good order.

By making smart choices about the way we furnish and care for our home, we can assure it will remain a place of comfort and safety for our families and avoid spending time and money on unnecessary things. This chapter will show you how to fill your home with the things that you love and how to be a responsible homeowner without overspending. The result will be less aggravation, less money spent on costly repairs and more time to devote to family.

Furnish Your Home for Less

When it comes to buying furniture, secondhand pieces are not only less expensive, they are often significantly higher in quality. Solid wood furniture made in the past is sturdier and more valuable than pressed-wood furniture sold today. Besides, secondhand furniture holds such interesting stories. I like to think about all the people who have used the furniture before it became a part of my home.

To get the best advice on furnishing a home most economically, I went straight to an expert. Connie Jo Tanner is a dealer of secondhand furniture. Here are her recommendations:

- *Estate sales are the best place to buy furniture and other home furnishings at bargain prices.* These sales are organized by professionals who are hired to clear the contents of an entire house. Unless stated otherwise, everything in the estate-sale house is for sale, including furniture, carpets, bedding, kitchen items and lamps. These sales are advertised in the newspaper.

Show up at the home and expect a crowd, as estate sales are well known for their treasures and bargains. Go with cash and a vehicle big enough to immediately take away what you buy. Always negotiate for a better price than what is marked. And for the best prices, visit the sale about two hours before it ends.

- *Secondhand and antique furniture stores are another ideal source for quality pieces.* These dealers buy their goods from auctions and estate sales. Although most items are reasonably priced, always negotiate. When the dealer gives you his best price, ask what his price would be if you paid cash and took it that day. Your willingness to remove it from the store immediately may be worth an extra 5 to 7 percent, as it frees the space for another item.

    If you don't find what you're after, let the dealer know. He will gladly take your name and number and call you if he finds it. Antique malls are another source for quality secondhand merchandise.

- *Buying and selling through classified ads is another source for home furnishings.* My family purchased beautiful, solid wood bunk beds for just $100 and a baby crib and dresser for $150. Five years later we sold the crib and dresser for $250, still a bargain price.

    Tanner cautions both buyers and sellers to be aware of the risks, however slight, that come with letting strangers into your home or with visiting a stranger's home. And know that some people will sell rental furniture to get quick cash. In this situation, you could end up losing the furniture and your money.

Pay Attention to Home Maintenance and Repair

In addition to buying quality furniture that will last beyond your years, it is important to take care of your other possessions so that they, too, will have a long and useful life. Living simply means being independent and self-reliant as much as possible. That includes keeping your home and all your possessions in good working order. Taking care of your home yourself, as opposed to calling a service for every repair, has benefits in addition to saving money. The knowledge you gain will serve you well in the future with other home maintenance projects.

Make Your Home Low-Maintenance

You can determine the amount of work required to keep your home clean and in good repair simply by the choices you make in furnishing it. Keeping your kitchen floor clean, for example, can be easy or a constant challenge, depending on the surface you select. Any surface with tiny indentations will trap dirt. White floors and cabinets are beautiful but absolutely impractical with children in the house. Ornate furniture traps dust in the grooves and can look dusty not long after being cleaned. Tables full of knickknacks take too much time to clean. (Remember, you could be playing basketball on the driveway with your kids instead.)

Want to keep it simple? As you furnish your home, think of how motels are furnished. Motel furniture touches the floor on all sides, leaving no chance for dirt or socks or toys to hide underneath. Arrange furniture so that your vacuum or dust mop can fit between the pieces. Make sure any new countertops are a smooth, solid surface instead of porous, like marble. If a remodeled bathroom is in your future, consider a suspended toilet, sink and soap dispenser. When they're attached to the wall instead of the floor, cleaning beneath them is a cinch.

Establish a Maintenance Routine

The simplest way to avoid home repairs is to establish a preventive maintenance routine. Here is a seasonal home maintenance calendar to help you do so. The month assigned to each task may vary for you, depending on where you live. Refer to the calendar frequently. If you tend to forget some things, like changing your furnace filter, add a note to your Master Calendar (see Chapter 1) as a second reminder.

Seasonal Home Maintenance Calendar

January

- Clean or replace furnace filter according to manufacturer's specifications.

February

- Have lawn mower serviced and blades sharpened.

March

- Clean and store sleds, snow shovels and other cold-weather equipment.

- Clean the garage. Dispose of old pesticides and paints. Ask your local public works department if you're not sure of the proper disposal procedure.
- Clean the grill (and check propane tank if gas grill). We use ours year-round, so it requires cleaning at least twice a year. But if you grill in warm weather only, now is the time to get it in good working order.
- Check bicycles for proper tire pressure. Make any needed repairs.
- Get other outdoor toys out of storage. (If you forget, your children will surely remind you.)

April

- Replace the batteries in your smoke and carbon monoxide detectors.
- Have your fire extinguisher inspected or replaced. Don't have one? Add it to your Wish List (Chapter 6).
- Replace storm doors with screen doors and storm windows with window screens. Clean screens first. I clean ours in the bathtub. It's easy if you have a shower hose. If not, clean them outside with the garden hose.
- Fertilize your lawn according to your weather zone. Northern lawns need fertilizing in spring and fall; warmer climates need fertilizing in spring early summer and early fall.
- Clean all ashes from fireplace. Put ashes in the compost pile.
- Clean gutters if within reach of your ladder. If not, arrange to have them cleaned.

- Have central air unit inspected according to manufacturer's specifications.
- Turn off your humidifier if you have one. Clean and drain per manufacturer's directions.

May

- Put garden hoses back on faucets. Inspect them for holes and bad washers.
- Get lawn furniture out of storage.
- Prune any trees with branches on or near your house.
- Wash windows. I use a professional squeegee purchased at a janitorial supply store. It makes an undesirable job a lot easier and faster.
- Inspect wood deck for loose boards and nails that have popped up. Apply a water sealer or wood preserver if water doesn't bead on the surface.
- Inspect roof vents and attic fans, making sure they are not blocked and are working properly.

June

- Wash aluminum siding with a mild detergent and garden hose.
- Make plans to paint any exterior surfaces that need attention.

July

- Use a garden hose to inspect the proper flow of water through gutters, downspouts and drainage pipes. (A broken pipe can mean water is draining into the ground and deteriorating your basement wall.)

- Use a vacuum to remove the lint from in and around your clothes dryer and on the refrigerator condenser coils for more efficient operation.
- If the heat of the summer has caused the soil to pull away from your home's foundation, water it regularly and/or add more soil.

August

- Clean all garbage containers, trash cans and recycling bins with detergent and the garden hose.
- Start to collect firewood from anyone who may be removing trees from their yard (this should be done through the end of the year).

September

- Clean or replace furnace filter according to manufacturer's specifications.
- Prepare humidifier for use during cold months.
- Arrange for a furnace inspection.
- Get out the squeegee and wash the windows again.
- Replace screen door with storm door and window screens with storm windows.

October

- Replace batteries in smoke and carbon monoxide detectors.
- Check your supply of firewood, road salt and snow shovels.
- Get sleds and snow shovels out of storage.
- Clean all lawn furniture with mild detergent, and store it.

- Arrange to have the chimney cleaned.
- Clean gutters if necessary.
- Prune tree branches that are touching or too close to the house.
- Seal and coat asphalt driveway.

November

- Do one final cleanup of debris from your lawn. Dead leaves will literally suffocate the grass and provide a place for leaf spores and disease to grow, leaving dead spots in the spring.
- Store bicycles and other outdoor toys.

December

- Vacuum refrigerator coils for more efficient operation.
- Collect, split and cut more firewood and kindling.

As you work toward a simpler lifestyle, remember that you want to spend as little time as possible caring for your home. The easier your house is to maintain both inside and out, the more time you'll have to enjoy your home and family.

Do It Yourself

There are plenty of reasons why doing it yourself is preferable. First is the money you'll save, which will ultimately enable you to spend fewer hours at work and more hours at home. Making repairs yourself also sets a wonderful example for your children. In a day when convenience is king, it's important for children to know that it's not always necessary to pay someone else to complete a task. Using the checkbook and the credit card can't compare with the satisfaction of learning how to do a job well and then completing the job yourself. With the proper amount of time devoted to it, a do-it-yourself project can also be a source of relaxation and enjoyment.

Two years ago I opted to paint all the outside wood trim on our home. I knew it could be a miserable job in the heat of summer, so I chose to do it during September, when the weather is much more comfortable in the Midwest. In addition to making sure I had all the right equipment before I began, I went a step further to make the experience pleasant. I gathered the portable tape player and all the old, homemade cassettes I recorded during my college days. Listening to those tapes made the job much more enjoyable. I felt like I was twenty years old again bounding up and down the ladder. In fact, I actually was sorry when the job ended.

Don't know how to do it yourself? Libraries are full of books, magazines and videos that explain almost any kind of home maintenance job. Several are recommended at the end of this chapter. The Internet is also packed with step-by-step advice for home repair projects. Although you'll find numerous do-it-yourself television shows, most of them make a job look way too easy, and assume you have more power tools than any family could possibly afford.

Some situations are best left to a professional. Ask yourself the following questions to help you decide:
- Do I have the right equipment, or can I borrow or rent it?
- Will the knowledge help me in the future?
- Would I rather spend the time with my family?

- Will I enjoy doing it?
- Can I be assured of my safety?

If the answer to any of these questions is no, hire somebody for the job, and spend your time on more worthwhile projects.

Decorate with the Things You Love

You can spend thousands of dollars on artwork created by people you'll never know to decorate your walls. Or you can spend almost nothing. From the time children enter kindergarten, they deluge parents with their own unique brand of artwork. Some of it is just "too cute" or "too clever" or "too inspirational" to throw away. So you put them in a box on a shelf and look at them only when you stumble upon them while cleaning.

Turn your home into a celebration of the people you love by decorating it with the artwork they have created. And I don't just mean the kids. Your mother-in-law's cross-stitch or your great grandma's hand-stitched quilt would make a beautiful wall hanging. Dad's first fishing pole could be a wonderful conversation piece hanging in the family room. Grandma's rolling pin collection or a piece of family china would add charm to any kitchen. Your parents' attic may hold a fantastic assortment of items to decorate every room of your home. Check your library for instructions on hanging delicate or cumbersome pieces.

Or turn a wall into a glimpse of your family genealogy. Gather all the old photos of your ancestors. Your grandparents' wedding photo or your dad's first-grade school picture are more meaningful than artwork by someone you've never met.

Although they may take a while to find, antique frames are best for old photos.

When they were young, my sister-in-law had her three daughters draw self-portraits using lots of colorful markers. She framed each portrait in brightly colored frames and hung them side-by-side in her kitchen. It was a clever way to brighten the room. If you can't find a frame in the size or color you prefer, order custom-made frames instead. Any how-to art magazine (check your library) will contain advertisements from mail order framing companies.

Filling your home with pieces of art or collectibles created by family is a simple, quiet way to honor the ones you love.

Resources

These three books come highly recommended by homeowners:

Home Book: The Ultimate Guide to Repairs & Improvements by Mark McClintock (Creative Homeowner Press, 2000)

50 Simple Ways to Save Your House by Bruce Johnson (Ballantine, 1995)

New Fix-It-Yourself Manual (Reader's Digest, 1996)

The Augustos—A Simpler Family

Back before the Augustos started living more frugally, their lifestyle was, as Denise puts it, discouraging. Despite two full-time incomes, Denise and her husband felt they simply couldn't have the things they wanted. They lived in a series of rather drab apartments with their two young sons and felt little sense of control over their financial circumstances.

They always felt that home ownership was out of their league. The couples they knew with similar incomes were able to buy their own homes with considerable financial help from relatives.

One day, after reading about couples who had developed a frugal lifestyle and were happy with the outcome, the couple set a goal for themselves. They would spend less and save for a down payment on a home. They continued to drive old cars, began cooking meals from scratch, shopped at secondhand stores, and ended up saving $3,000 the first year. The following year, Denise quit her home day-care business to concentrate on their goal of home ownership.

In spite of their reduced income, now $26,000, the next year they saved another $7,000 and had their down payment. During this time, Denise read how-to books on home purchasing, fine-tuned her tightwadding skills, and together with her husband decided exactly what kind of home they wanted—lots of space for the kids, new construction, and something within a twenty-minute drive of Marte's job.

After looking at a dozen homes, they found a six-year-old house with slate floors, on seven wooded acres, surrounded by hundreds of acres of state forest in Northfield, Massachusetts. It was only ten minutes from Marte's job. The previous owner's marriage had dissolved, and the house had been on the market for a couple of years, so they managed to buy it for nearly $15,000 below the asking price. Shortly thereafter, when Marte brought a friend on a tour of the house, his friend said, "I can't believe you can afford a place this nice." Denise agrees. "Almost four years later, I still get a thrill every time I pull into the driveway."

The Augusto children are by no means deprived, even though they don't wear designer clothes. In fact, a scaled-back lifestyle has really rubbed off on them. Their nine-year-old thinks his friends who wear only Nike or Tommy Hilfiger clothes are slightly nuts. And their thirteen-year-old frequently puts off purchases to "wait until tag-sale season starts again."

"We now feel more confident of our financial abilities, and we don't worry about money, because we know that with creativity, we can manage," reports Denise. Living frugally has enabled them to spend money on the things they truly value. Their youngest, for example, has a $500 mountain bike. He is bike-obsessed, rides year-round, and sometimes races, so they feel the purchase was a good value.

They are also more goal-oriented. After deciding to purchase a home computer, they quickly put several hundred dollars toward that goal. During the next several months, they plan to research their purchase, decide what will work best for them, and save enough to buy what they want.

Denise is now working as a teacher's aide while her children are in school. But she is always home when they are home. "It's funny," she reports, "living on less money has made us a happier family!"

CHAPTER 5

Leisure Time, Vacations and After-School Activities

"Rest is not idleness, and to lie sometimes on the grass on a summer day listening to the murmur of water, or watching the clouds float across the sky, is hardly a waste of time."

—*Sir J. Lubbock*

THESE DAYS, IT SEEMS that afternoons spent dreamily reading a book, playing in the sandbox or running through the sprinkler are nearly extinct. As parents, we feel an obligation to expose our children to as much as possible. But in doing so, we eliminate the possibility of our children quietly learning on their own.

It's not just the children whose calendars are overbooked. When we aren't running the children here and there, we parents face a lengthy to-do list of our own. Our "spare time" isn't spare. Instead, we are busier during our free time than we are at work and spend our weekends hurriedly running from one place to the next in order to get everything done. Somehow we feel guilty taking a nap or reading a magazine because it isn't "productive." So we go, go, go, but our destinations somehow don't make us especially happy.

Simpler families make spare time their own. They refuse to spend their free hours in the car. They opt, instead, to spend this time at home simply relaxing with family.

The ideas that follow will show you how to slow the pace of your family life. They will help you rediscover the tremendous joy of a schedule whose only demand is that the family spend more time together.

When Children Get Home from School

For families with both Mom and Dad working, it can be difficult to have a parent at home when the school bus arrives. It's possible, however, after implementing some of the ideas presented in this book, that at least one parent can work fewer hours in order to be home after school (see Chapter 9). I've found this is the time of day when problems at school or problems with friends are most likely to come spilling out. I've certainly witnessed my share of meltdowns at this crucial hour. But an hour or two later the problem may have drifted to the back of my child's mind—until it surfaces the next day at school as an even bigger problem. After school is also the time when children are most eager to share the good news about a grade, a project or some other exciting event.

One morning, when my daughter was in first grade and I was still working full time, just minutes before the morning bus was to round the corner, she said, "Oh, I'm supposed to dress like a Pilgrim today." She got on the bus in tears, and I felt bad all day at work. Avoiding situations like this is the purpose of establishing a brief after-school routine. The routine at our house works like this: before the children arrive I clear the kitchen table, get out the cereal (their favorite after-school snack), bowls, spoons and milk. I insist they sit down with me for ten minutes, eat their cereal and discuss anything important that happened in school or on the bus. I ask how much homework they have and whether there is any big event at school the next day. This helps me help them schedule enough evening time to prepare for the next day.

If any of the after-school conversation requires a lengthy discussion, save it for dinnertime. This gives the other parent a chance to participate too.

Homework

When and where to do homework is a hot topic of discussion among the experts. Here are some general guidelines:

- Make sure there is no television within earshot.
- If you permit the student to accept phone calls during homework time, make sure they are brief. And do not allow calls to be made unless they pertain to schoolwork.
- Allow frequent breaks, depending on the child's ability to focus for extended periods of time.

- Write the due dates for important projects on your Master Calendar (Chapter 1) to make sure deadlines are met. In addition, encourage your student to keep track of project deadlines on a wall calendar in her bedroom.

At our house we reserve homework until after dinner. I personally think the kids deserve a break after being in school all day. But when it's time to settle down and get to their work, we don't set many rules. They can work at the kitchen table or at the desk in their room, wherever they feel most productive. They know it is their responsibility to get their work completed before bedtime, and they decide where they can best accomplish the task.

After-School and Evening Activities

A growing chorus of experts is warning of the dangers of over-scheduling a child's life. They believe that a child's after-school activities should not consume every last bit of Mom and Dad's time, money and energy. They further believe that such over-scheduling is not only bad for parents, it's potentially dangerous for the healthy development of the child.

I am in wholehearted agreement. I once returned home from a hectic evening of taking children to and from activities and insisted they start their homework. They replied, "But we didn't get any time to play!" It was then that I realized the frenetic after-school pace was as exhausting for them as it was for me. What they really wanted was downtime to relax and do as they pleased.

With their child's best interests in mind, many parents cross the line from reasonable to ridiculous when it comes to involvement in sports. A child who excels in soccer could be content to play on the neighborhood team. Instead, parents (sometimes with the urging of their child) seek a spot on the city's "select" team, including an aggressive schedule of practices and games. Weekends are consumed by traveling, sometimes hours from home, not only for the player, but for his parents and siblings, too.

Before registering your children for next season's activities, ask yourself, and your children, the following questions:

- Are you enjoying the activity?
- Are you learning something through your involvement?
- Are you participating because your friends are doing it, because you think Mom and Dad want you to, or because you want to?
- Is your schedule making unreasonable demands on the rest of the family?
- Would you rather stay home and play Monopoly?

Richard Carlson, author of *Don't Sweat the Small Stuff with Your Family,* warns that children who have too many opportunities, choices and scheduled activities "expect to be entertained and stimulated virtually every moment of every day." Eventually they need a television, radio, video game, telephone or computer to entertain them every moment of the day. Believing that boredom encourages creativity, Carlson thinks parents do their children a favor by teaching them that there's nothing wrong with not having something to do.

In addition to the time after-school activities require, most also carry a hefty price tag. Beyond registration fees, there are event fund-raisers, coach's gifts and fast food because there's no time to cook. Family dinners, quiet evenings at home, uninterrupted play with the neighbors, extra time for homework . . . it all gets set aside. Reconsider your child's activities, and you may find that you could make a change that makes everyone happier, including your child.

Mealtime as a Celebration

Christmas dinner, Passover seder, and Thanksgiving dinner are all occasions that call for celebrating with food. Such celebrating can be done on a day-to-day basis, too. Evening dinner is the rare chance a family has to be together and should be considered as important as a holiday meal. But for many families, it is an endangered event.

Not only is dinner an important time to regroup as a family, it's good for family health, too. A study from Cincinnati Children's Hospital Medical Center showed that children who ate with their families at least five times a week were less likely to use drugs or become depressed than those who ate with their parents just three times a week. Researchers at Tufts University found that the less often people of all ages ate out, the less body fat they had, the fewer calories and fat they consumed, and the more fiber they consumed.

Dinnertime is an opportunity to relax, to interact with family members, to share some laughs and to make plans. The payoff is tremendous. In her book *Kids Are Worth It!,* longtime educator Barbara Coloroso states, "If you can get your young children to talk with you at meals, they will still talk to you when they reach the teen years, since they will have learned that mealtime is a safe time for sharing."

Starting Discussion

If your children aren't willing to enter into a discussion during mealtime, try this approach, practiced by one of my neighbors. Each evening during dinner everyone, including Mom and Dad, must answer this question: "What's the best thing that happened to you today, and what's the worst thing that happened to you today?"

By scaling back afternoon and evening activities for children as well as parents, you'll find it much easier to gather everyone together for dinner. Be flexible, taking into account the schedules of everyone involved. If someone has practice until 7:00 P.M., make mealtime 7:30 P.M. that day. Or schedule dinner at 5:30 P.M. to accommodate a 7:00 P.M. meeting. Gathering everyone together every evening may not always be possible. But with some added effort, and by making dinnertime a priority, daily family dinners can become a reality.

Establishing a few mealtime rules is a good idea. Here are some possibilities:

- No reading the paper or looking over the mail
- No answering the phone
- No negativity—this is supposed to be enjoyable
- No headphones

- No radio or television

When I grew up, dinnertime was a daily, mandatory event. I can vividly recall all eight of us kids packed around a turquoise padded bench—this was the early seventies—eating Mom's special meatloaf. We called it Meatloaf Monday. I don't recall what dishes were synonymous with the other days of the week, but I remember that dinner at home was a loud, happy family event. Maybe that's why it's so important to me today.

Evenings

If you would like to spend more evenings at home with family, then make a conscious effort to see that it happens. Some evenings are dictated by sports practices and PTA meetings, but if you follow the advice presented earlier in this chapter, you will soon be spending more quiet evenings at home with a family that is happy to be there. Make a conscious effort to keep your evenings simple, and everyone will become happier and more relaxed.

We keep a jigsaw puzzle set up on a card table in our family room at all times. I think of it as a calming force if an evening gets stressful with homework. And puzzles are a great educational activity for kids. How gratifying to see a puzzle completed, knowing the entire family had a hand in creating it.

When my husband and I both worked full time, I often felt guilty about hurrying the kids to bed in the evening. It seemed we barely spent any time together before it was time to go to bed. So we started a nightly contest of Crazy Eights. Each evening we played a game or two and posted the winners on a chart taped to the refrigerator. It was a wonderful, calming nighttime routine that made settling into bedtime a little easier. Maybe your kids are a little older and Crazy Eights doesn't sound like much fun. You could try playing some of those board games that are stacked in your closet. One quick family game of Clue can be the perfect nightcap to a family's hectic day, much more enriching than half an hour of True Hollywood Stories or Cops.

My friend Donna Collins started a nighttime ritual she called "Happy Thoughts" to keep her four-year-old from having bad dreams. Each night at bedtime, Mom, Dad and Son discussed the happy things they had done during the day. Their hope was that by sharing happy thoughts, their son would have more pleasant dreams. This calming routine put an end to bad dreams.

Weekends

For many families, a typical Saturday goes something like this:
- Up by 8:00 A.M.
- No time for French toast. Eat a granola bar in the car instead.
- Swing by gourmet coffee shop on the way to son's basketball practice.
- After practice, run into Toys 'R Us for birthday party gift.
- Stop home for forty-five minutes.
- Take daughter to ballet.
- Everyone's hungry. Go to McDonald's for lunch.
- Daughter wants to go home, but son wants to stop by the mall for newest Gap pants. Fight ensues. Son wins. Grumpy

daughter decides she wants eight-dollar bottle of shower gel. You buy it just to keep her happy. Buy Gap pants and return home for an hour.

- Drive son to birthday party, and then pick up daughter's friend so they can play.
- Return home.
- Girls complain they are bored and want to go to a movie. You get the picture.

Days like this leave everyone feeling ragged and the wallet empty. It would be a lot more fun—and less expensive—to spend Saturday preparing a nice homemade brunch, sipping coffee, reading the paper, and watching cartoons. After you discover just how much fun it can be, you won't want it any other way. Your children won't either. Try some of the ideas here, and watch the bond between family and friends strengthen.

Home Is Where the Fun Is

To most Americans, our home is our castle. We spend lots of time, money and energy making it comfortable and attractive. Yet most families don't relish the idea of spending their weekends at home and do everything they can to avoid it. Most families spend their weekend hours shuffling kids from place to place—the movies, Discovery Zone, the amusement park, the batting cages. Try some of these at-home activities instead:

- Make your neighborhood the site for Friday night volleyball games and cookouts. When the weather is bad, host Friday night card games or board games instead. Get competitive if you like. Let the winners keep coveted homemade trophies until the next Friday.

- Turn your driveway into a city block. Using chalk, draw "roadways" on the driveway, wide enough for a Big Wheel or tricycle. Let the kids do the rest, making a gas station, grocery store, bank and so on out of boxes.

- Suggest to younger children that they make their own grocery store. Stock it with items from your pantry. Encourage them to make signs, price tags, and play money. Our basement was a grocery store for months when the kids were younger. Eventually it became more special with an old cash register donated by my brother, who was upgrading to newer models in his stores. Later, after Santa brought the kids a blackboard, wall maps and a pointer (get these at a school supply store), the basement became a classroom.

- Do your children actually play with the toys you carefully selected and purchased for them? Or are their rooms full of items they don't have time to enjoy? It may take some initiating on your part, but with a little nudging your children will realize how much fun they can have with what they already own. Suggest the kids gather every toy car and truck they own and create an enormous city. They can spend an entire day making roads and buildings.

- Remember lemonade stands? Kids can spend half a day preparing for and selling lemonade. Painting and hanging posters, setting up tables and chairs, gathering supplies and finally selling lemonade is not only fun but a good lesson in economics, too.

- Challenge every child or family in the neighborhood to build a tent in the backyard made from bedsheets or blankets, and then enjoy a neighborhood camp-out.
- Play dodge ball, pickle, or Ghost in the Graveyard. Share some of the favorite at-home activities from your childhood with your children.
- The next time you have an old television or other small appliance that's ready for the trash heap, let your children take it apart instead. My son spent two days tearing apart an old television and then took the most interesting pieces to school for show-and-tell. Note: remove the electrical cord completely before they get started.
- A few years back, I painted a checkerboard on a small table that sits on our front porch. Black and grey rocks, collected from a trip to Lake Michigan, became checkers. When the weather is nice, my kids and I play checkers while they wait for the bus. It's a pleasant way to get the day started.
- Instill a spirit of charity in your children by doing something nice for others. It can be as simple as walking around the block, or through the park, picking up trash. Visit an elderly neighbor.
- Pull out your boxes of family photos and get everyone involved in organizing them into albums.
- Instead of sleeping in, get up with the sun and tend to your garden while the rest of the world is still in bed.

Look through your home with a fresh eye. Challenge your family to spend an entire weekend without leaving home. In time, they may not want to go anywhere else.

Places to Go—for Free

When the family is eager to leave the house, try some of these inexpensive ideas.

- Too often the library gets thought of as the place to do research for a school project. But libraries are also packed with videos, DVDs, CDs, cassettes and magazines absolutely free to borrow. Libraries are one of my all-time favorite places to spend a spare hour—especially on Friday evenings when it's nearly empty and we practically get the whole place to ourselves. Going to the library is a wonderful way to spend a simple evening with your family and promote learning at the same time.

- Once you attempt to reduce your spending, you'll uncover all sorts of things that are free. Look into these:
    - Lots of museums are free on Saturdays (with special activities for kids).
    - Events like county fairs are sometimes free during the days if you arrive early.
    - Your park district may provide lots of free activities. Contact them, or check your newspaper.
    - Many Friday newspapers list free activities for the kids during the upcoming weekend.

- Although some hobbies are expensive, others are free and fun for the entire family. One weekend, grab some binoculars and try birdwatching at the park. Bring a library book to identify birds, a jar for bugs and a notebook to record what you see. If your family enjoys the day, and you are successful in spotting a few different birds, bring your supplies along on your next vacation. You might find birds in another state that you wouldn't in your own. If you have trouble finding any interesting birds, look for other critters instead. And enjoy the hike.

- Not all college sporting events cost money to enjoy. Take the family to a free event, and cheer for the home basketball or football team.

- Explore your state with your children during a long weekend, or see how much you can pack into just one day. Here's an example:

  Living close to the Ohio River, I knew our state was home to a series of locks and dams designed to keep the water level at a set height without affecting river traffic. But I had never seen them operate and always wondered how they worked. I was pretty sure my children would find them interesting, too. So, one summer morning we packed a lunch, hopped in the car and drove to the closest dam, more than an hour away. Standing on a platform watching an enormous barge squeeze into one of the locks was fascinating to observe. We stayed for more than an hour, watching big boats and little boats take their turns moving up and down the river. It was a beautiful day and a great learning experience, and it didn't cost a dime. As a bonus, we stumbled upon the birthplace of Ulysses S. Grant on the drive home.

- Follow the advice of Cincinnatian Thom Jackson. After too many overbooked weekends with not enough time for family, he instituted "Wide World Jammy Day." Once a year, he and his two children spend the entire day in their pajamas playing at home together with no interruptions allowed.

- It may seem like an unusual way to have fun, but visiting a cemetery can bring history alive. Larger, older cemeteries usually have self-guided tours available to show where famous persons are buried. It may be a bit spooky, but it will definitely be educational, too. And it's a great reminder to live life to its fullest.

- Have fun people-watching. If it's a nice day, go to a park to simply sit and watch the people go by. If the weather won't cooperate, try a bookstore or mall. Browse the stores, and have fun watching the busy shoppers. Just be careful not to buy anything.

- Have chores to do? Don't dread them; make them fun, instead. As mentioned in Chapter 4, listening to your favorite tunes will make any job more enjoyable. Bruce Springsteen is my favorite bathroom-cleaning companion.

My husband and kids regularly turn the job of raking leaves into a family production. The kids string together a series of plastic sleds and hook them to a toy tractor to carry the leaves to the curb. Then they dump them and return to the backyard to start all over again. The kids enjoy it, and the yard work gets completed all at the same time.

Here's one more example of how what adults might consider "work," kids would consider "play." At tax time I was busy getting our files in order. My son (age eight) was looking for something to do and asked if he could help. So I handed him the stack of gas and electric bills and told him to make a month-by-month chart. How much did we spend on gas each month? Why did we use so much gas in the winter? Why didn't we use a lot of gas in March? How much did we spend on electricity? How much did we spend the entire year? Not only did he enjoy the job, he learned a lot about how our household expenses work, too.

Vacations

Vacations are time with family. They don't need to be expensive. Exotic or opulent destinations aren't remembered as long—or as fondly—as a unique shared experience.

Every family has its own idea of what a simple, uncomplicated, relaxing vacation is like. For us, it's driving to a beach and staying in a hotel. Many families like to go camping. Collecting firewood, cooking outdoors, roasting marshmallows, hiking and sharing a tent is a wonderful family adventure.

Whatever you consider "vacation," here are a few ideas for keeping it an enriching family experience:

- Make "getting there" part of the fun. Leaving at midnight and forcing a sleepy parent to drive through the night can result in one cranky family upon arrival. Leave at a more reasonable hour, and plan to have some fun along the way. Look in your library for books full of car games. Our favorite: give everyone a map of the United States and a crayon. When you see a license plate from a particular state, color in that state. At the end of the trip, the person with the most states colored wins.

- Borrow a copy of the book *Watch It Made in the U.S.A.: A Visitor's Guide to the Companies That Make Your Favorite Products* by Karen Axelrod and Bruce Brumberg (John Muir Publications, 1997) from your library. It's a comprehensive listing of factory tours, many free, organized by state. You may find you can take a quick tour, learn something new and take a break from the road all at the same time.
- Keep a vacation journal, or write funny poems about memorable vacation events. Display them in a photo album with your vacation pictures for long-lasting memories. Here's a poem my eight-year-old son wrote about a particularly memorable experience during our vacation in Hilton Head, South Carolina:

> *We rode bikes to the beach,*
> *And then we came back.*
> *Then I got sick,*
> *And threw-up in the bath (room).*

- Instead of taking the fastest route, travel the back roads. Stop at roadside diners; visit vegetable stands. Talk to the people who live there about their town. It's more educational and fun than driving the interstate and eating fast food.
- If there's room in your hotel, bring a jigsaw puzzle and work on it together during downtime.
- Rent bikes, or take your own, and explore beyond the confines of your hotel or campground.

Regardless of your plans, just make sure the vacation is time spent together as a family. Don't put the kids in a day camp while the parents play golf and tennis all afternoon. Family vacations are meant for families. If you want to take a special golf or tennis trip, do it another time, without the kids.

Ideally, you'll return from your vacation feeling happy and rested and closer as a family unit.

CHAPTER 6

Parties, Gifts and Holidays

"There's no place like home."

—Dorothy, Wizard of Oz

BIRTHDAYS AND HOLIDAYS are opportunities for us to gather with family and celebrate a special occasion, often with gifts and special meals. But amidst all the commercialism that surrounds these occasions, we easily forget the real reason we're celebrating. We spend, spend, spend. We cook and bake until it's no fun anymore. And we buy gifts with little meaning to fulfill the obligation. In the end, we make it a celebration others expect it to be instead of one that will make our family happiest. We exhaust ourselves and our budgets, when what we would really prefer requires a lot less energy and expense.

This chapter will help you to slow down and rediscover the meaning of your celebrations. Follow the advice, and you will plan birthday parties that are fun, not frenetic. Your holidays will be filled with simple pleasures, meaningful gifts and the joy that comes from being with family.

Birthdays

The simplest of families has a tendency to abandon its good senses when it comes to celebrating a child's birthday. Birthday parties are held to celebrate a birth, to say "we're so glad you are with us" and "we're grateful for another healthy year." But somewhere between the frantic pace of the roller rink and the mound of presents to be opened, we lose sight of the reason for celebrating in the first place.

Elaborate birthday parties cost elaborate amounts of money. With thirty-plus kids at the roller rink and so many presents that they don't get opened until after the party ends, the birthday child gets cranky from all the attention. Hundreds of dollars later, the cranky birthday host sends his guests on their way with a four-dollar goody bag full of stuff that will probably be thrown away in a matter of days.

Birthday parties don't have to be complicated, nor do they need to cost a bundle. Some of the best I've seen cost next to nothing, and the kids had a wonderful time. Here are my recommendations for simple, meaningful, enjoyable parties.

- *Invite only the child's closest friends, not the entire class.* That way everyone has time to enjoy each other's company. A common recommendation is to limit the number of guests to the age of the child, but even that can be too many. Trying to keep eight children entertained can be overwhelming to a child turning eight years old. He may be more comfortable with just three of his closest friends.

- *Don't plan a formal birthday party every year.* Limit parties to ages five, eight and ten. On the other years, have the neighbors over for an impromptu cupcake or ice cream bar on your front porch. This gives some recognition to the birthday child without the time and expense of a big party. It also relieves friends of buying presents every year.

- *A "reverse surprise party" is the simplest, and perhaps the most sincere, form of celebration.* It is held during a gathering of friends, perhaps at school or during sports practice or church. The birthday child tells no one it is his birthday. At an appropriate time during the gathering, the child announces the surprise: it is his birthday, and he wants everyone to help him celebrate by sharing a piece of birthday cake. No invitations, no presents, no party favors, no thank-you notes. Just a surprise, a song and a piece of cake.

On years when a formal party is on the agenda, brainstorm with the birthday child for inexpensive ways to celebrate. Here are a few of my favorites:

- Have all the kids wear boots and spend the afternoon at the creek. Bring a bucket for any creatures they might collect.

- Organize a touch football or soccer game at the park. Give the kids colored scarves for their heads, or come up with some other inexpensive way to indicate the two teams.

- Have older kids arrive in the evening and then build their own tent in the backyard (or inside if weather is inclement).
- If the neighborhood is safe, send the kids on a scavenger hunt.
- Make up a dance to a popular song, and then put on a show.
- Play a couple of board games, or break the group into teams and make up your own quiz show.
- Working in teams of two, give the kids makeup and hair accessories, and then challenge each team to create the most unattractive look.
- Give each child a clue written on a piece of paper in lemon juice. In order to reveal their hidden clue, they must hold their paper over a lightbulb until it's warm enough for the message to appear. All clues lead to a hidden treasure box.
- If a special event is taking place at the library or the park, make it part of the party.
- Host a "Backward Birthday Party." Write invitations backward. Have everyone wear their clothes backward, sing "Happy Birthday" backward, and hold their fork backward while eating cake.
- Make it a "Purple Party" (or your child's favorite color). Make purple invitations, have guests wear as much purple as possible (give a prize for that), and make all of the plates, cups and prizes purple. Even the cake can be purple! Let the whole family search for purple things to do at the party, like pin the tail on the purple donkey.
- If planning an adult birthday party, ask everyone to come to the party prepared to complete the following poem with words describing the birthday person:

Roses are red,
Violets are blue,

_____

_____

Regardless of your party plans, be sure to get invitations in the mail two to three weeks in advance. Mark your Master Calendar (see Chapter 1) so you won't forget to do so. It's best not to have invitations distributed at school to avoid hurting the feelings of those not invited.

A Note About Thank-Yous

Insist that your child send a note of thanks to everyone who gave him or her a gift, no matter how small. Notes should go to children as well as adults, relatives as well as friends. Anyone who spent the time to make or purchase a gift or write a birthday check deserves a written thank-you.

Christmas and Other Gift-Giving Holidays

Imagine a perfect Christmas. You might envision giggling children gathered under the tree, eager to open the two presents Santa left for each of them, followed by a simple family dinner where everyone enjoys just being together. Unfortunately, Christmas morning for many families means agitated children, exhausted from tearing open a dozen presents and still looking for more, followed by a complicated family dinner with too much food, a frazzled cook, and an hour's worth of dishes to clean afterward.

If you wish your holiday were more about peace on earth and goodwill toward all and less about shopping, cooking, cleaning and wrapping, here are ideas for making it happen.

First, proceed slowly. As Jo Robinson and Jean Coppock Staeheli warn in their book *Unplug the Christmas Machine* (Quill, 1991), altering family traditions, even if they aren't especially satisfying, can be difficult. There is comfort in familiarity, and other family members may not be eager to make the changes you suggest. Proceed slowly, looking upon the next holiday season as the first in a five-year plan. Then you will have the patience to make small initial changes.

Begin by thinking about all the activities that go into preparing for the holiday:

- Write a gift list.
- Buy presents.
- Wrap presents.
- Compile a holiday card list.
- Buy cards.
- Sign, address, stamp and mail cards.
- Help out at school parties.
- Plan holiday gatherings, and finalize plans.
- Dig out the traditional family recipes.
- Make special grocery shopping list.
- Prepare meals.
- Buy Christmas tree or Hanukkah decorations.

- Dig out holiday decorations that are in storage.
- Decorate inside of house.
- Decorate outside of house.
- Mail any out-of-town gifts.
- Agonize over whether you spent the same amount on each child.
- Buy last-minute gifts.
- Attend holiday functions.

Now carefully consider each activity, and jot down ways in which they can be simplified, or even eliminated. Carefully planning the holiday in advance is a worthwhile step. Before December is upon you, plan the entire month. Make room for family-only days, which allow for such simple pleasures as driving through the city to enjoy the lights. Encourage quiet time during the busy season: peaceful walks, frequent naps, periods with no television or computers. Start a simple holiday-eve tradition that takes the focus away from presents: take the family outdoors and generously spread birdseed to make sure the birds have a happy holiday, too. The holiday you plan should be one that is meaningful for your family, not one that others think you should have.

Simplify Gift Giving

Buying gifts is perhaps the most stressful, time-consuming and costly activity associated with the holiday season. The television commercials, store displays, mail order catalogs, and radio and Internet ads are all in full swing by mid-October. And each time we see or hear one, we are reminded of the shopping tasks that lay ahead.

It doesn't have to be this way. First, make a conscious effort to walk away from the television commercials, avoid the store displays, cancel mail order catalogs (see Chapter 1) and tune out the ads on the radio and the Internet. Next, put more meaning (perhaps more fun) and less expense into gift purchases. As the saying goes, "It's the thought that counts," not the amount of money you spend.

These ideas might work for you:

- Suggest to family members that gifts be given only to children.
- Instead of buying gifts for everyone in your extended family, institute an exchange of names so that you buy for only one adult, child or couple instead of everyone.
- Instead of an expensive gift exchange, have a white elephant gift exchange. Everyone in your extended family or workplace brings something they already had around the house (or purchased at a garage sale).
- Put a three-dollar limit on gifts for adults. It can be challenging, fun and actually more meaningful than a fifty-dollar item.
- Buy a copy of your favorite book for everyone on your list. Make it meaningful.
- Skip the gift exchange with friends, and plan an evening out to dinner instead.
- Instead of purchasing a gift, write a thoughtful letter expressing your love and admiration for the recipient. Wrap it in a nice box.
- Give your time as a gift. Present it as a gift certificate to be redeemed during a less hectic month, such as a homemade

dinner, a lunch date, a complete car cleaning or baby-sitting. You will need to make certain your offer is redeemed, as the recipient may be hesitant to do so.

- In lieu of exchanging gifts, make a group donation to a favorite charity.
- If a membership to the YMCA, the museum or the zoo is something your family desires, yet is beyond your budget, be honest. Ask for a contribution toward your "Join the Zoo" fund.
- Give homemade gifts instead of store-bought gifts. See the ideas later in this chapter.

Simplify Meals

Have Grandma's walnut, raisin and cornbread stuffing and Great Aunt Sarah's luscious nectar cake always been a part of your holiday dinner? Would Christmas just not be Christmas without it? If you are hosting the meal and family tradition demands certain dishes be a part of it, be sure to ask for help in preparing them. Assign the cake to your sister and the dressing to your mother, and don't feel guilty.

In November, when you sit down to map out your December, plan the "other" meals that are a part of the holiday. Prior to the holiday season, prepare simple meals that are short on preparation and long on relaxation, like the ones recommended in Chapter 2. The result will be a less hectic week with more time to enjoy family.

Big holiday dinners can leave everyone feeling stuffed, cranky and less than eager to start the dishes. Rather than watch everyone dragging their bodies from the table to the couch after the meal, suggest a spirited game of basketball in the driveway or a stroll around the neighborhood instead.

Simplify Decorations

To some, decorating the home for the holiday season is a two-hour project. For others, it can take two (or more) days. Climbing up and down the ladder to hang the newest brand of chasers, icicles and other fancy lights takes a lot of time and energy, not to mention money. I'm grateful for the people who are willing to put in the hours and expense of these elaborate decorations. Driving around and enjoying the lights is a tradition for many families.

But if decorating the house is a job you would love to eliminate, consider this. Sometimes the simplest decorations are the most attractive. They're less costly, too. Hang a wreath on your door, and position a spotlight nearby. Or place an electric candle in every window of your home. These are simple decorations with beautiful results.

Make holiday decorations in such a way that your children can participate. Contrary to the message they hope to send, most holiday magazines are packed with photographs of gorgeous homemade decorations that clearly did not include a child's touch. It is sad, because children are the ones who get the most enjoyment from them.

Put more meaning into decorating your home for the big event by asking your children to help. The final result doesn't have to be picture-perfect. If your children are old enough to climb the ladder and hang lights along the gutter, show them your confidence by letting them complete the job. Who cares if the lights are a little droopy?

The Christmas tree doesn't have to be symmetrical with lights evenly spaced, garlands perfectly placed, and fragile ornaments flawlessly hung. Somehow a tree that is slightly off-kilter, with ornaments hung only as high as a child's hand can reach, seems much more "perfect."

Decorating our house with a homemade, life-size Santa is one of our traditions. For several years we had him sitting on the rocking chair on the front porch, a spotlight heralding his presence. This past Christmas we hung Santa from the windowsill of our son's bedroom instead, supposedly peeking inside to make sure someone was "nice instead of naughty." It was a fairly amateurish job (some of the neighbors didn't realize he was peeking inside and thought he was washing the windows instead). But it's a great family activity, so the tradition will continue.

Extend the decorations beyond the living room by giving each of your children a strand of lights to hang in their bedrooms, in any manner they prefer. They'll fall off to sleep at night in the glow of twinkling lights, excited and grateful for your confidence in their decorating abilities. Give them each a sprig of mistletoe as well!

Make Your Own Ornaments

Use your sewing machine to make Christmas tree ornaments that evoke memories using old baby blankets, childhood clothing, or fabric that includes a school or scout emblem. Here's how:

1. Use heavy cardboard to make a cutout of a star, diamond or other shape.
2. Trace the cutout onto two pieces of fabric, and then cut the fabric into the shape you've drawn.
3. Putting the good sides of each piece of fabric together, stitch around all but one section of your star or other shape.
4. Turn the fabric right-side out, and stuff with inexpensive batting found in fabric stores.
5. Place a piece of looped ribbon into the opening (to hang your ornament once completed), and then stitch the final section.

Simplify Holiday Cards

Holiday cards can be a wonderful way of staying in touch with faraway family and friends. They've been serving this purpose since the 1800s. But with December's to-do list already so lengthy, you might find holiday cards easy to eliminate. Many families no longer send them. We certainly don't receive as many as we used to, and I don't think poorly of the families who have stopped.

If cards are important to you, here are few ways to simplify the process:

- Here's how we keep it simple. Sometime during the fall, we make a big sign that says "Happy Holidays from the Kleins," then take black-and-white group photos around the sign. Once photos are developed, we select our favorite and then have a printer make 50 photocopies on heavy paper the size of a postcard. In all, it costs us $25 plus postcard postage.

- An alternative idea would be to skip the Christmas greeting and send Happy New Year cards instead. These can be done during the quieter days between Christmas and New Years, or even extend into early January, whenever you find yourself with a little more time. Or wait until February and send personal Valentine greetings instead. I know one Irish family who extends St. Patrick's Day greetings in lieu of Christmas cards.
- Limit the number of cards you send, or simply decide not to send cards at all. You will enjoy crossing one more task off your to-do list, and it's possible no one will even notice.

Lower Your Expectations

When we think of Christmas, we often imagine happy, well-behaved children enjoying each other's company; the family gathered around the tree singing carols while watching the snow fall; a beautiful midnight church service where the kids sing joyfully and quietly fall asleep in the car afterward; and a handful of perfect gifts for the children, every toy working properly, with no returns needed. As every honest parent knows, this Christmas is a fantasy. As you anticipate the next holiday season, be realistic about what you can (and cannot) expect. If you expect perfection, you'll most certainly be disappointed.

Thanksgiving

Compared to Christmas, the Thanksgiving holiday is relatively unscathed with commercialization. It's simply a day for giving thanks, watching football and eating. Preparations typically fall on the host, who must clean the house, dig out the china, and purchase and prepare the food. If that is you, lighten your load by asking every guest to bring a part of the meal. If mashed potatoes or dessert are the things you least like to prepare, assign them to someone else.

In her book *Family Traditions* (Reader's Digest, 1992), Elizabeth Berg recommends drawing names for teams to work together once the guests arrive: one team is in charge of setting the table, another for clearing it, another for doing the dishes, another for serving dessert. This gets everyone in on the act and saves the cook from collapsing at the end of the feast.

In the spirit of the season, Berg recommends playing "Alphabet Thanks" as the meal begins. It is a clever way to get everyone involved in expressing his or her gratitude. During the meal, have each person say something for which they are grateful. The first person mentions something that begins with the letter A, the second person mentions something that begins with a B, and so on. If done quickly, the game can be both fun and easy for everyone.

Unfortunately, some families feel obligated to celebrate the holiday at two different homes, consuming two Thanksgiving meals. One generous couple I know encourages their children, all married, to enjoy the holiday at their in-laws' homes. The following Saturday, free of other obligations, the couple and their children gather for their own celebration.

If you spend Thanksgiving with family but miss celebrating with friends, start a new tradition. In mid-February, when most families are less busy, host a Thanksgiving meal for all your friends. Like the original Thanksgiving, be sure to ask everyone to contribute a dish to take the burden off the host.

Favorite Gift Ideas

When purchasing gifts for children, it is best to give things that will stimulate their imaginations as opposed to things that require them to simply sit and observe. Here are a few ideal gift ideas:

- *Children under five:* Office supplies (index cards, paper clips, pens, hand stamp with ink pad, inexpensive calculator, tape, glue) so they can pretend they're at work; blackboard, chalk, eraser and maps to play "school"; homemade blocks in lots of shapes and sizes (be sure to sand rough edges); primary dictionary; a book; dress-up clothing and jewelry

- *Six- to ten-year-olds:* Preprinted return address labels; a hammer, nails, wood scraps; an electric pencil sharpener; a date with one or both parents (no siblings allowed); a gift certificate to office or art supply store; large bottles of tempera paint, brushes and poster board; a bulletin board; a book

- *Preteens:* A blank journal with fancy pen; any clothing with name of high school they'll attend or their favorite college; a disposable camera; a photo album; an autograph book; notepads preprinted with name and address; a book; a magazine subscription; a jigsaw puzzle; a board game; a CD or cassette

- *Teenagers:* A share of stock; tickets to an upcoming sports event or concert; a gift certificate to the mall; a gasoline card; any clothing from a favorite university; a book; a magazine subscription

Make-It-Yourself Gifts

Any gift-giving celebration, whether birthday, anniversary, Hanukkah or Christmas, is more meaningful when the gifts are homemade.

I often hear of families who exchange only gifts they made: canned tomatoes from backyard gardens, a photo album, hand-crafted baby blocks, muffins from scratch. Such homemade gifts carry a special meaning. Unfortunately, during a hectic holiday season, most families don't have the time it takes to work on homemade gifts. But if crafted during other less-busy times of the year, handmade gifts can be completed and then stored until the appropriate occasion.

- Purchase inexpensive clay pots, and have your children paint colorful designs on each. Put your compost (Chapter 2) to work by planting an herb or spring bulb in each pot. Give one larger pot for a sunny location on a porch or deck, or three small pots for the windowsill.
- Make pretzel dough (see recipe) and ask your children to form interesting shapes. Bake and store in a colorful can or basket.

Pretzels

2 cups warm water
2 packages yeast
⅓ cup sugar
2 teaspoons salt
¼ cup soft margarine
2 eggs
Approximately 6½ cups flour
Coarse salt

Put water in a large, warm bowl. Sprinkle in yeast. Stir. Add sugar, salt, margarine, 1 beaten egg, and 3 cups flour. Beat until smooth. Add enough additional flour to make stiff dough. Cover bowl tightly with aluminum foil, and refrigerate for anywhere from two to twelve hours.

Dust a cutting board with flour. Take half of the dough and divide into handfuls. Have your children roll the dough into strings, slightly thinner than a pencil, then loop the dough into various shapes. Place on a greased baking sheet. Brush pretzels with the remaining beaten egg. Sprinkle with coarse salt. Bake at 400 degrees for fifteen to twenty minutes until light brown.

- Make a garden marker, the perfect gift for a gardener. Find a nice, smooth stone. Using permanent, oil-based paint, carefully paint the words: "Grandma's Garden" or "Charlotte's Garden." Children under ten may have a difficult time painting the words, so let them choose the stone, and you can do the painting. An alternative is to paint the same words on a piece of wood, then nail a stake to the wood so it can be pounded into the earth in the recipient's garden.

- Homemade bubble bath is easy to make and a joy to receive. Using a kitchen grater and a bar of Ivory soap, make 1 cup of soap flakes. Add 1 cup of water and 3 tablespoons of glycerin. If desired, add scent with a few drops of essential oil, and color with one or two drops of food coloring. Store in a decorative bottle with a cork top. Instruct the recipient to shake before using. Shelf life is two to three months. (Glycerin and essential oils are available at large health food stores.)

- Stationery is always a nice gift, especially when it is lovingly decorated by children. Purchase heavy drawing paper or watercolor paper from an art supply store and plain white envelopes (note card size) from an office supply store. Cut and fold the paper to fit the envelope. Older children can use stencils or sponges and paint to decorate the front of the cards. Younger children can decorate with stickers, markers, watercolors or potato prints. Tie six note cards and envelopes together with ribbon. Slip a nice pen into the package if you like.

Sponge painting is simple. Use scissors to cut a cellulose sponge into a favorite shape (hearts are easy). Make several sizes of the same shape if you like. Use pieces of leftover sponge. Dip the pieces lightly in your favorite color tempera paint, and then dab onto a paper towel to remove excess.

Lightly press the sponge onto your card. Practice on scrap paper first until you get the feel of the process.

Potato prints are made using the same technique. Using a sharp knife, an adult should cut a potato in half, then carve the raw end into a favorite shape. Dip the potato into tempera paint, and transfer to cards as described above with sponge painting.

- Young girls especially enjoy fruit-flavored lip gloss. And it is simple to make. Add 2 tablespoons of petroleum jelly to 1 teaspoon of powdered fruit drink mix. Stir together, and microwave until well blended (about twenty-five seconds on high). Transfer to small jars or plastic containers found in drug or beauty stores. Refrigerate for twenty minutes until solid, and then remove from refrigerator.

- Anyone with a fireplace appreciates receiving firestarters as a gift. If they are homemade, they are appreciated even more. Here's a simple way to make firestarters that will make the house smell warm and cozy: Melt paraffin wax on the stove in a double boiler. Once completely melted, add cinnamon oil, vanilla oil, or another favorite scent. Reduce heat. Tie sturdy cotton string to the center of a pinecone. This string will be the firestarter's wick. Holding the string tightly, dip the pinecone into the melted wax until it's completely covered. Let cool on waxed paper.

Wrapping Paper

Part of the fun of receiving a present is tearing apart the wrapping paper. It's one of life's pleasures, especially for kids. At our house we always take the time to wrap a present and include a ribbon. But the cost is next to nothing. I purchase wrapping paper only when it is extremely cheap (sometimes during the holidays you can find big rolls of plain blue paper on sale, which can be used year-round). Otherwise, we use plain white paper and decorate it with markers, stickers, or sponge or potato printing. Have a giant roll of butcher paper in the house at all times. We keep a roll in the corner of our kitchen and use it not only for wrapping paper, but for school projects, art projects, happy birthday signs and lemonade stand announcements.

Made-in-Advance Greeting Cards

With all the extra leisure time your family will have after following the advice in Chapter 5, you will never have to purchase a greeting card again. Making cards, whether for Valentine's Day, birthdays, anniversaries, thank-yous, or to attach to a gift, can be so much fun. On a lazy day, gather all the markers, paints, papers, sponges, brushes and other art supplies, and go to work. Put on some music, and spend an hour with the kids creating blank cards appropriate for any occasion.

Simpler holidays and family celebrations do not come about easily. To be successful, you must make a plan and have the fortitude to stick to your plan.

- Identify what is most important about the celebration: family togetherness and a simple gift exchange, for example.
- Eliminate everything that is not important: elaborate decorations and a complicated meal, for example.

- Do the best you can throughout the celebration, and the days leading up to it, to emphasize what you have determined to be important.
- Don't expect miracles, particularly the first year you try to simplify.

Simplifying celebrations isn't always easy, especially when the media and well-meaning friends encourage us to do otherwise. By implementing some of the ideas in this chapter, and by having the strength to say no to the expectations of others, future celebrations can be simple, peaceful, enjoyable, inexpensive, meaningful and fun. Take small, determined steps. Your family will love the results of your efforts.

The Berghoffs—A Simpler Family

The Berghoffs are a simple family in many of the ways described in this book. They live in a nice home in a nice neighborhood, but they are happy to live without the luxuries common to their neighbors. Doing so enables them to live on the income from Tim's business, where he works about twenty-five hours a week as an actuarial consultant. Kathy stays home with their three children, ages eight, six and two.

One of the ways the Berghoffs live simply is by owning just one television. And instead of keeping it front-and-center in the family room like in most homes, the Berghoffs' television is kept in a sparsely furnished, spare bedroom on the second floor of their home—no stereo sound and no cable. "Just whatever we can pick up on the old rabbit ears," says Tim.

The kids spend just thirty minutes a day, prior to bedtime, watching an age-appropriate program that Kathy taped earlier in the day. The rest of the day, instead of sitting in front of the tube, the Berghoff children are reading, playing games and talking with each other. "Our kids have a unique ability to entertain themselves creatively," Tim explains. The average American, on the other hand, watches three hours and forty-six minutes of television a day, adding up to fifty-seven days a year.

Living without a television so central to their lives makes the Berghoffs more aware of the background noise it creates in other homes. "I hate to walk into someone else's house and hear the television noise all the time. It's irritating," says Tim. The only time Tim and Kathy truly miss their television is on those rare occasions when some big news occurs. "Then it is mildly inconvenient to go upstairs to watch the news coverage for a bit."

Unfortunately, minimizing television has not made the Berghoff children less interested in specific toys and brands of clothing popular with other kids. They may not own it, but they still want it.

Tim and Kathy are pleased with the way their out-of-the-way television has simplified family life. The disadvantage: "We cannot host a Super Bowl party!" is Tim's reply.

CHAPTER 7

Health

*"The best piece of advice I could give anyone is
pretty simple: Get a life. A real life, not a manic
pursuit of the next promotion, the biggest paycheck,
the larger house."*
    —Anna Quindlen, A Short Guide to a Happy Life

A RECENT STUDY INDICATED that people suffering from high
blood pressure and other stress-related diseases often complain
of having little control over their lives. Their world is spinning
out of control, and they can't seem to stop it. This is true as well
for those of us without high blood pressure. But we have to
remember—our life is in our control. Our health is, too, and the
simpler our lives are, the healthier our family will be.

The slower pace of simpler living leaves room for healthy routines like exercise, relaxation and proper nutrition, which have proved to increase longevity and keep health problems at bay. But good health also requires attention to preventive measures. Thousands of studies, some cited throughout this chapter, have proved the lifelong benefits your family can enjoy by keeping in good health. This means you can save hundreds of dollars in health insurance costs over the course of a few years.

The Food Guide Pyramid

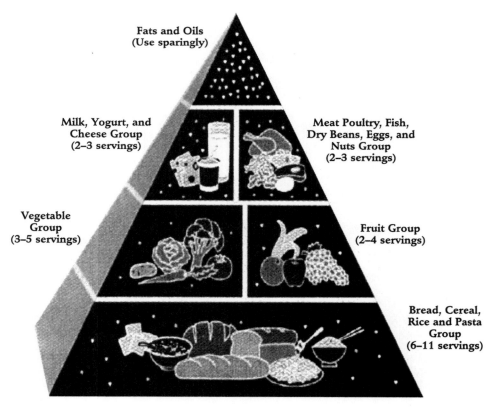

Fats and Oils
(Use sparingly)

Milk, Yogurt, and
Cheese Group
(2–3 servings)

Meat Poultry, Fish,
Dry Beans, Eggs, and
Nuts Group
(2–3 servings)

Vegetable
Group
(3–5 servings)

Fruit Group
(2–4 servings)

Bread, Cereal,
Rice and Pasta
Group
(6–11 servings)

Source: U.S. Department of Agriculture

Eat Right

As early as the first grade, children are introduced to the Food Pyramid. We know we should eat lots of whole grains, eat five fruits and vegetables a day, go easy on the meat and dairy products, and eat sweets and fats sparingly. Yet our hectic schedules mean we can be found at the drive-through window more than ever before. Burgers, nuggets, fries and sodas don't fulfill the guidelines set forth in the Food Pyramid. Instead, these high-fat, high-cholesterol foods can lead to serious health problems.

If the idea of improving your health doesn't motivate you to eat right, consider doing so for the sake of your children. If you show your children how to eat right by providing them with only healthy foods, you'll be laying the groundwork for their long and healthy lives, and the lives of your grandchildren too. Although it isn't always obvious, your children rely on your guidance.

Here's a sample menu, for one day, that fits all the guidelines set forth in the Food Pyramid.

Menu for Children

Breakfast: 1 cup cereal, 1 cup milk, ½ cup fruit juice

Lunch: 1 half turkey or bologna sandwich, celery with peanut butter, two oatmeal cookies, ½ cup milk

Dinner: ½ cup raw or steamed vegetables, ½ cup fruit salad, ½ cup pasta with marinara sauce, one small piece French bread, ½ cup milk

Snacks: Bagel or muffin, carrot sticks with ranch dressing, 1 cup ice cream

Menu for Adults*

Breakfast: ½ bagel with jelly (men and teen boys, whole bagel), one piece fruit or ½ cup fruit juice, 1 cup yogurt or milk

Lunch: Turkey, tuna or egg salad sandwich with lettuce and tomato or cucumber; celery with peanut butter; one piece fruit or ½ cup fruit juice; carrot sticks

Dinner: ½ cup raw or steamed vegetables (men and teen boys, 1 cup), ½ cup fruit salad (men and teen boys, 1 cup), 1 cup pasta with marinara sauce, one small piece French bread (men and teen boys, two pieces)

Snacks: Bagel or muffin, four crackers with 1 ½ ounces cheese: men and teen boys add 1 cup ice cream and hard-boiled egg

Setting a Good Example

You can alter the eating habits of your entire family by making simple changes. For example, if a typical breakfast for your children is a bowl of Apple Jacks or a Frosted Pop Tart (each of which contains more grams of sugar than a Reese's Peanut Butter Cup), explain to them how too much sugar affects their ability to pay attention throughout the school day. A piece of fresh fruit and toast or whole grain cereal will have a more positive effect on learning. Follow through by refusing to purchase sugar-laden breakfast foods, and model for them a healthier way to begin each day.

Providing your family healthy, wholesome meals can have lifelong positive effects. Here are some simple ways to improve

---

* assumes coffee, tea, diet soda or water as beverage

overall family health. If making all the changes at once seems overwhelming, choose one or two each month.

- Eat no more sugary cereal for breakfast.
- Check the labels on other "breakfast food" (like doughnuts and breakfast bars). How nutritious are they?
- Insist on eating fresh fruit every morning with breakfast and a fruit and vegetable every day with lunch.
- Use only whole wheat flour in pancakes, breads and muffins.
- Pack a nutritious lunch every day instead of buying lunch (see Chapter 2).
- Make sure after-school and after-work snacks are nutritious and won't ruin dinner.
- Plan dinners that are nutritious. By following the advice in Chapter 2, you'll find this easier than it sounds.
- Limit fast food to once a week (less often is even better).
- Drink at least twenty-four ounces of water between every meal.
- Pay attention to the amount of sugar in the foods you currently eat, and then reduce that amount. Even fruit-flavored yogurt is high in sugar. Check the labels on the foods you eat, and choose low-sugar foods.

Family Mealtime

One of the easiest ways to be healthy is to eat together as a family. According to the American Dietetic Association, children who eat regularly with their families tend to have healthier eating patterns that contain more fruits and vegetables and less fried foods, soda and saturated fat compared with those who do not eat regularly with their families. They also have a higher intake of calcium, iron, fiber and vitamins—all of which are important for children's growing bodies. By simplifying the work-and-activities schedule for every member of the family, as recommended in Chapter 5, family dinnertime can be a reality.

In addition to the mealtime rules included in Chapter 5, these ideas will help ensure that dinnertime is a positive family ritual at your house:

- Turn off the television and radio so conversations won't be distracted.
- Let the answering machine pick up calls.
- Discuss positive events of the day or upcoming family activities. One family I know asks every family member to say the best thing and the worst thing that happened to them that day.
- Remember that kids sometimes take more time to eat than adults do. Take your time, and enjoy the extra few minutes sitting at the table before cleaning up.

How Television Affects Our Food Choices

We all know that being a couch potato doesn't do much for the physique. But what we may not have considered is the effect of television commercials on our food choices. (How often do you see a television commercial for raw carrots or tap water?)

The U.S. Department of Agriculture conducted a study that showed the more television a child watches, the more likely that child will consume the foods advertised on television, foods that are more likely to be high in calories. Further, the American

Heart Association found that television commercials for high-fat foods make up 41 percent of total commercials shown on Saturday mornings.

So, in addition to all the other reasons cited throughout this book for reducing the amount of television viewed in your house, you can add this one: it encourages you and your children to consume foods that aren't good for you.

Exercise

Eating right is one way to avoid health risks and stay in control of your family's health. But it is equally important to be physically active. Most experts recommend that you and your children try to get at least thirty minutes of physical activity into each day. It doesn't have to be complicated or expensive. You don't have to join a gym, buy a treadmill or run a marathon. You simply need to try and exercise half an hour a day.

A walk at lunch and a family basketball game in the driveway before dinner are excellent habits to instill in your family. Running with the dog, roller-blading, swimming, sled riding and ice-skating are all preferable to sitting in front of the television or computer. Make exercise a regular part of your family's day. The next time you need to go to the library, try walking or riding a bike instead of driving.

What is keeping your children from being active—the television, the computer, the feeling that they need to be driven to the park or the gym? Encouraging your children to play outdoors (or insisting, if necessary) will get them moving. Join them whenever you can. Just as you model good food choices by healthy eating, you display good free-time choices by exercising.

Medical Checkups

Keeping yourself and your children healthy is just as important as getting treatment when you or they are sick. Regularly scheduled checkups will save you money in the long run by preventing minor problems (caught during checkups) from becoming major—and more costly—problems down the road.

The Agency for Healthcare Research and Quality recommends the following immunizations:

- *Polio (OPV/IPV):* At 2 months, 4 months, 6–18 months, and 4–6 years.
- *Diptheria-Tetanus-Pertussis (DTaP):* At 2 months, 4 months, 6 months, 15–18 months, and 4–6 years.
- *Measles-Mumps-Rubella (MMR):* At 12–15 months and either 4–6 years or 11–12 years.
- *Haemophilus Influenzae Type B (Hib):* At 2 months, 4 months, 6 months, and 12–15 months; or 2 months, 4 months, 12–15 months, depending on the vaccine type.
- *Hepatitis B:* At Birth–2 months, 1–4 months, and 6–8 months. If missed, get 3 doses starting at age 11 years.
- *Chickenpox (VZV):* At 12–18 months. If missed, get between ages 11 and 12 years.
- *Hepatitis A:* At 24 months–12 years in selected areas.
- *Pneumoccoccal disease (Prevnar™):* At 2 months, 4 months, 6 months, and 12–15 months. If missed, talk to your health care provider.

Children aren't the only ones who need to see a doctor regularly. It is recommended that healthy adults receive a physical checkup once a year. Women should get a pap smear every year and a mammogram every three years between ages twenty and thirty-nine, every two years up to age fifty, and then once a year. Be smart. If your cholesterol is high, have it rechecked frequently, as advised by your physician. Or if your mammogram is not conclusive, have it rechecked as your physician advises. If you are being treated by a physician, he or she should tell you when to schedule a follow-up appointment.

Both children and adults should see a dentist every six months, not only for a thorough cleaning, but for a thorough inspection for cavities, cracks, or other tooth and gum damage. If left undetected, such problems won't go away. Instead, they'll become painful and costly. Encourage good dental hygiene when your children are young, and you'll see far-reaching effects. This includes twice-a-day brushing, every-other-day fluoride rinses (available at any drug store) and daily flossing. I became a fan of flossing when, after years of costly dental work, my husband and I began flossing daily. Since then (it's been years) we have had just one cavity between us. If you think a Water Pik or electric toothbrush would result in better dental hygiene, make the purchase. The cost should be quickly recovered in lower dental bills.

Insurance

The reason we carry health and dental insurance is to help us pay for a portion of the cost of care. But as we well know, not all expenses are covered.

As painful as it may be, read your insurance policy carefully. You'll learn what is excluded, but you might also learn of benefits you didn't know you had. Sometimes a dentist, for example, will recommend a treatment that is not covered under dental insurance. But a check of your health insurance policy may indicate that it is covered through that provider instead.

You should be aware of the exclusions and limitations of your health plans, but you shouldn't let those factors alone determine your decisions about treatment. Make smart choices. As previously mentioned, living simply doesn't always mean spending less money.

A Year in Advance

At the start of every year, make all necessary doctor and dental appointments for every member of the family. Mark each appointment on your Master Calendar (see Chapter 1) so you won't forget.

Sleep

If you have ever had a restless night with very little sleep, you probably recall how it affects you the next day. It makes you drowsy and cranky, not the loving parent you want to be. But according to the American Medical Association, lack of sleep can create much more serious consequences. In 1999 they reported that the inability to get a refreshing night's sleep may actually slow your recovery from an illness and can lead to emotional or mental problems.

The most common sleep-related complaint is insomnia. About 30 percent of American adults suffer from it, at least occasionally. They complain of the following:

- Having difficulty falling asleep
- Waking up frequently during the night with difficulty returning to sleep
- Waking up too early in the morning
- Experiencing unrefreshing sleep

Insomnia leaves parents feeling tired, lacking energy, having difficulty concentrating and feeling irritable during the day. Any of these symptoms can put a strain on a happy family life.

Children Need Sleep, Too

Adults aren't the only ones who need a good night's sleep in order to function properly. A team of Northwestern University scientists found that two- and three-year-old children sleeping less than ten hours in a twenty-four-hour period were consistently at greatest risk for behavioral problems such as aggression, "acting out" and noncompliant behavior.

Preteens also need their rest. The American Psychological Association recently reported that sixth-graders often suffer adverse cognitive, behavioral and emotional consequences when they are chronically sleep deprived. On the other hand, because second-graders tend to get one full hour additional sleep than sixth-graders, they typically do not display morning drowsiness or daytime sleepiness.

If anyone in your family suffers from poor sleep, try the recommendations listed here before going to the expense of seeing a physician or sleep specialist:

- Let your body determine how much sleep you need. The amount varies with each individual. For some, three or four hours are adequate, while others need nine or ten to feel rested. Most adults need about eight hours. If you aren't getting enough sleep, your body will tell you. You will fall asleep easily while watching television or feel sleepy throughout the day. If this sounds like you, try sleeping longer to determine if that helps. On the other hand, if you have a difficult time falling asleep, perhaps you're trying to force your body to get more sleep than it actually needs.
- Get up about the same time every day.
- Go to bed only when you are sleepy.
- Establish relaxing rituals before bedtime, such as taking a warm bath or reading.
- Exercise regularly, but do so at least three hours before bedtime. People who exercise regularly report getting more restful sleep and sleeping more deeply than those who do not.
- Maintain a regular schedule.
- Don't eat a big meal just before bedtime.
- Don't eat or drink anything containing caffeine within six hours of bedtime, including soda, decaffeinated coffee, iced tea, and semisweet chocolate.
- Don't drink alcohol within several hours of bedtime or when you are sleepy. Although it may help you fall asleep quickly, it tends to disrupt normal sleep patterns, preventing you from getting the restful sleep you need.
- Don't nap close to bedtime.
- If you take naps, try to do so at the same time each day.

- Don't self-medicate with sleeping pills. You might soon find yourself unable to fall asleep without them. Instead, try one of the home remedies listed at the end of this chapter.

Reduce Stress

For many busy parents, stress is a normal state of being. They've had a life filled with stress for so long, they know of no other way to live. They don't recognize the toll that stress is taking on their bodies and on other family members. (One recent study showed that family stress has an adverse affect on the sleep patterns of sixth-graders, leading to drowsiness during the school day.)

Although there is such a thing as "good" stress that actually makes us perform better, most stress is "bad" and can actually make us sick. Calling stress "America's number one health problem," the American Institute of Stress reports that 43 percent of all adults suffer adverse health effects due to stress. And 75 to 90 percent of all visits to primary care physicians are for stress-related complaints or disorders. The bottom line: a life filled with stress is both dangerous and costly.

Eliminating stress is one of the biggest benefits of a simpler lifestyle. By scaling back, you will free yourself of the self-imposed stress of keeping up with the neighbors, the stress of rushing from here to there to here again, the stress of planning major birthday and holiday extravaganzas, and the stress of being unorganized and out of control. Instead, you will experience the joy of doing what you and your family truly desire, not the hectic life that others expect and impose upon you.

Simply by following the advice presented throughout this book, you will reduce your stress and become more in control of your life and the lives of your family. Here are other ways to eliminate stress in your everyday life:

- Stop trying to do it all. Recognizing that you are capable of doing just one thing at a time, and being unwilling to take on more than you can reasonably handle, will automatically reduce the level of stress associated with a hectic family life.

- Get rid of the cell phone, or give yourself periods of the day when it will be turned off. With it, you run the risk of being interrupted even during precious downtime (like when you're driving in the car singing your favorite oldies). You don't really need to be accessible twenty-four hours a day.

- If listening to the constant drone of television causes you stress, then place some limits on it. I typically allow my kids to watch television every morning for half an hour while they wake up and eat breakfast. But after one particularly quarrelsome morning, I decided no television for a week. What a difference! It was a very calm week.

- Avoid medication to control your stress, unless advised by your doctor. Try some of the ideas in this list and throughout this book before resorting to costly (and sometimes addicting) medication.

- Get in the habit of exercising whenever you feel tense. Feel like screaming at the children? Take them for a bike ride, or play a quick game of soccer with them instead. Then see if you feel better.

Home Remedies

Visits to the doctor for regular checkups and serious illnesses are crucial to a healthy family. But you don't need to see the doctor for every little cold, ache and pain. Before scheduling a doctor's appointment or purchasing an over-the-counter medication, try these home remedies:

Insomnia

- Drink a glass of pure, warmed grapefruit juice just before bedtime. If necessary, sweeten it with honey.
- Drink of cup of chamomile tea and take a warm bath before climbing into bed.

Head Cold

- At the first sign of a cold, drink a cup of echinacea tea with honey.
- Eat hot, spicy foods. They make your nose run, which is said to trigger glands that produce cold-fighting antibodies.
- Drink hot homemade chicken soup, especially one that includes garlic, curry or hot pepper as an ingredient.

Sore Throat

- Put a pinch of curry in warm chicken broth and drink when symptoms first appear.
- Gargle with warm saltwater every few hours. Do not swallow the rinse.

- Mix equal amounts of hydrogen peroxide with warm water, and gargle every few hours. Do not swallow.

Earache

- Carefully put three drops of warm (not hot) olive oil in affected ear. Plug with cotton. Note: this remedy is not to be used if the ear is discharging fluid or if an ear tube is in place.

Swimmer's Ear

- If experiencing minor pain after swimming, mix 1 teaspoon of white vinegar with 4 tablespoons of just-boiled water. Once cool, store in a clean bottle. Insert two drops in affected ear just after swimming. Plug with cotton for five to ten minutes.

Poison Ivy

- Mix 1 tablespoon of baking soda in a bowl of warm water, and soak the rash.

Bee Sting

- First, remove the stinger by scraping the skin with a credit card or other blunt object. (Pulling it straight out may squeeze the stinger's sac, releasing more venom.) Then apply either (1) ice, (2) a paste of baking soda and water, (3) antiperspirant containing aluminum chlorohydrate, or (4) household ammonia. All have shown to reduce the pain and itching.

Healthy Routines

Here are other simple routines that will promote good health in your family:

- Use sunscreen daily on exposed skin.
- Drink water instead of soda and juices. When their children were very young, my neighbors kept a sports bottle filled with water on the bottom shelf of the refrigerator for each child. They always had a cold drink within their reach, and now they are accustomed to drinking water regularly. It is cheaper and healthier.
- Choose biking or walking over other forms of transportation. Walk to the mailbox. Pick the parking spot that is farthest from the entrance to the grocery store. Bike to the library or any destination that is less than a mile away.
- Encourage frequent hand washing throughout the day.
- Insist everyone wear helmets when biking and skating.
- Lighten up! Solid scientific research now proves that a good belly laugh boosts the body's immune system and reduces hormones that cause stress.

To maintain good health and keep health care expenses to a minimum, you must take control of the way you treat your body. Living at a slower, more manageable pace, eating the right foods, and exercising regularly will have lifelong benefits for your entire family.

CHAPTER 8

Major Expenses

"There's no reason to be the richest man in the cemetery. You can't do any business from there."
Colonel Sanders

IN PREVIOUS CHAPTERS we have reviewed ways to trim a few dollars from various parts of the family budget; here are opportunities to save hundreds, even thousands.

It is not uncommon for people to make a special trip to a store to save one or two dollars for an item they need or will need in the future. We think it's worth it sometimes to go out of our way to save a few bucks. But when it comes to the biggest expenses in our life, like insurance, for instance, we don't seem to pay as much attention. By simplifying your life, you'll have more time to evaluate the items that cause the biggest drain on the family budget. And by doing so, you'll uncover ways in which you can save not just a dollar or two, but hundreds (even thousands) of dollars.

Insurance

The purpose of insurance is to protect you and your family in the event of a catastrophe. You don't need insurance to pay for every minor bump in life's road. If you are buying your own health insurance (as opposed to receiving it as a benefit of employment), be sure it will prevent your family from falling deeply into debt should a disaster occur. But don't pay for coverage you don't need.

Most of us obtain our medical insurance through an employer. We aren't shopping for the best rates and determining the best coverage. But when it comes to insuring our cars and our homes, the "shopping" becomes our responsibility. There are better ways to spend your money (see "Wish List" in Chapter 6) than for insurance coverage you don't need.

Once you have simplified your life and have more time to review your major expenses, shop for car insurance first. More than 45 percent of Americans never shop around for auto insurance, although premiums for policies offering identical coverage vary widely from company to company—as much as $500 for six months of coverage. After hearing this statistic, I shopped around the next time our car insurance was up for renewal. With my current policy in hand, I made a few phone calls and ended up with a new, identical policy that saved our family $500 a year.

Ironically, our old policy included a "discount" because the coverage was with the same company as our homeowner's policy. Here are some typical ways to save on auto insurance:

- Forgo personal injury protection, which pays for the medical and funeral costs associated with an accident for you and your family, regardless of whose fault it was. If you have separate life, health and disability policies, these expenses are probably already covered.

- Choose the highest deductible you can afford on collision and comprehensive coverage that pays for repairs or car replacement. If you have an older car, drop the coverage altogether.

- Don't take the extras, like rental car reimbursement and towing coverage.

When you have the time, review your homeowner's policy, too. Does your policy include private mortgage insurance? PMI is generally required if the down payment on your home is less than 20 percent of your home value. But once you've paid off 20 percent of your home value, you no longer need the insurance. Be sure you aren't paying for insurance you no longer need.

The best way to save on homeowner's insurance is to do your homework. By shopping around, you can save 25 percent or more. Typically the lowest rates available are from companies selling insurance directly over the phone rather than through agents. Check your yellow pages for such companies.

Life Changes Mean Changes in Coverage

As you get older and your children move out of the house, you don't need the same amount of life insurance you did when they were babies. And as your automobiles age, consider the cost of each type of coverage. It doesn't make sense to pay for collision and comprehensive coverage (which can account for up to 40 percent of your total premium) for a six-year-old automobile.

Transportation

The simplest of families needs a vehicle to get everyone where they need to be. It doesn't need to be as big as a house. It doesn't need to cost a fortune in gasoline and insurance. It shouldn't put the family in deep debt. And it doesn't have to be the newest model. Yet it needs to be reliable and well maintained. Put simply, we need something that will transport the family safely and effectively.

If you want to reduce your overall expenses, your family transportation is a good place to start. I'm not suggesting you live without (although some people maintain that a one- or no-car family is ideal). You can own two cars without draining your bank account. The advice that follows will show you how.

New or Used? Lease or Purchase? Cash or Credit?

You can find an argument to support any of these options. Some would say new is best—you know exactly what you're getting. Others argue that used is better—let someone else pay for the depreciation. Fans of leasing think it makes the most sense—the down payment is minimal, and the monthly payments are cheaper. Still others contend that if you purchase the car, you'll drive it for years without making a payment once it's paid off. Can't decide? Do your homework:

- Read the safety reports for automobiles you're considering. You'll find them at the library or on the Internet.
- Decide how much you want to spend.
- Determine which options you need.
- Calculate the cost of insurance for each car you're considering.
- Compare the gasoline usage for each car.
- Use free Internet sites to determine dealer cost, to see car reviews and to price your trade-in.

Even if you can comfortably afford a new car, look at how much money you might save buying a used car. For example, if you purchase a used minivan for $20,000 instead of a new sport utility vehicle for $40,000, then take the $20,000 you save and invest it at 8 percent compound interest, you'll have $29,797 in five years, or $44,393 in ten years. That's enough to pay for a college education.

Once you have decided on the car you want, do more homework. If you are buying new, look in the New Car Cost Guide at your library or on the Internet to find out the dealer's invoice price and the manufacturer's suggested retail price. Decide what you think is a fair profit for the dealer—$300 or so. Then visit a dealer and indicate what you want and how much you'll pay.

If you prefer to buy a used car, check the N.A.D.A. Official Used Car Guides in your library. You'll learn the value of the car you're considering, as well as the value of the car you might be selling or trading in. The Internet has various free sites that also provide useful information.

Paying cash for your car will save you a significant amount. The following chart indicates how much your loan will end up costing you, depending on the interest rate and the length of the loan. If you can't pay cash for the entire amount (most people can't), consider putting down as much cash as you can comfortably afford.

A Four-Year Loan

Amount Borrowed	Total Payments at 7% interest	Total Payments at 8% interest	Total Payments at 9% interest
$5,000	$5,747	$5,859	$5,973
$10,000	$11,494	$11,718	$11,945
$15,000	$17,241	$17,577	$17,917
$20,000	$22,988	$23,436	$23,890
$25,000	$28,736	$29,295	$29,862
$30,000	$34,483	$35,155	$35,834

The most important lesson is one my family learned the hard way: don't ever be in a hurry to buy a car. Don't wait until your old car can barely make it out of the driveway. Don't wait until a week before your family vacation to start looking. Anticipate your needs, and allow two months for shopping, or you will likely end up buying more options than you want and paying a higher price than you should.

Take Care of Your Investment

Regardless of which car you own, or your method of obtaining it, you must take good care of it.

- Change your oil frequently.
- Rotate tires regularly.
- Keep tire pressure where it should be.
- Have maintenance work done in a timely fashion, before small problems become major.

And don't drive your car if you don't have to. A nice walk is as good for your car as it is for you and your family.

Utilities

Unless you're living on solar energy, you can't forgo paying a monthly utility bill. Living simply still requires gas and electricity. But you can take some steps to reduce the amount of energy your family uses.

The following chart is a good indicator of which household appliances are running up your utility bill. Although the price for a kilowatt-hour (kWh) fluctuates depending on where you live, this chart, based on a price of eight cents per kWh, will help you target areas for savings.

Electrical Appliance	Typical Wattage	Operating Cost
Air conditioner		
Window unit	1,208	10 cents/hour
Central unit, three ton	5,400	$345/year
Clothes dryer	5,000	40 cents/hour
Curling iron	80	0.64 cents/hour
Dishwasher with heater	1,200	9.6 cents/hour
Freezer, upright, 15 cu ft		
with auto defrost	580	$11.40/month

Electrical Appliance	Typical Wattage	Operating Cost
Hair dryer	1,200	9.6 cents/hour
Microwave oven	1,500	12 cents/hour
Range		
large surface unit	2,700	21.6 cents/hour
oven unit 350 degrees		16 cents/hour
Refrigerator/freezer		
14 cu ft, auto defrost	440	$10.60/month
20 cu ft, auto defrost	500	$13.70/month
Television, color	180	1.4 cents/hour
Vacuum cleaner	500	4 cents/hour
Washing machine	500	4 cents/hour

Household Appliances—Approximate Cost of Operation courtesy of Cinergy Corp., Copyright 1996–2001. All Rights Reserved.

With a wife, eight children and various animals all living in a modest four-bedroom home with only one full bath, I can still recall my dad being frustrated with keeping our family energy consumption to a minimum. The hot water heater (which uses more energy than any appliance in the house) was always working overtime, as we each remained in the shower until a sibling came knocking—for the second time. With ten people in the house, there wasn't a lot we could do in the way of saving energy, other than keeping the refrigerator door closed, keeping our showers short, turning off "all those blasted lights," and closing the door behind us—"We're not heating the backyard, you know!"

Today, as he and Mom relax in their condo by the lake, Dad surely laughs whenever he hears one of us shouting at *our* kids to "close the door!" Because, as we have reached middle age, we have finally learned. It may not make a huge difference, but when it comes to saving energy, every little bit helps. With that in mind, here's a list of some of the little things you and your family can do to save our planet's precious resources—and a few dollars too.

- Turn off the water while shaving or brushing teeth.
- Keep the furnace filter clean (mark your Master Calendar for every six months).
- Adjust the thermostat when everyone is sleeping or not at home. (An automatic thermostat will do this for you. They cost less than $100, are easily installed, and can save you up to 35 percent on your energy bill.)
- Thaw frozen food in the refrigerator.
- Keep the freezer full (it will run more efficiently) by using frozen cans of water if necessary. They'll come in handy when you need to fill the cooler with ice.
- Caulk windows and door frames to seal cracks.
- Set your hot water heater at 120 degrees. Most are preset at 140 degrees.
- Close vents and shut doors in rooms you don't use.
- Keep fireplace flue closed when not in use.
- Limit showers to five minutes.
- Wash clothes in cold water.
- Air-dry clothes that take a long time to dry (like blue jeans). Once dry, toss them in the dryer for a few minutes to soften them.
- "Turn off all those blasted lights!"
- Close the door behind you. "We're not heating the backyard, you know!"

Housing

Your home can be a tremendous source of comfort and pride. Compared to other costs of living, it is also a tremendous expense. But there are steps you can take to keep the cost of homeownership to a minimum.

Size

As the saying goes, your home may be your castle, but an enormous home can also be a hindrance. The cost of energy is one reason. Owners of very large homes typically pay two to three times the cost for gas and electricity as owners of more modest homes. Cathedral ceilings and rooms that are rarely used are costly to heat and cool. Big homes also require more furniture, more carpet, more landscaping and more stuff. And the more "stuff" you have, the more "stuff" you need to clean, repair and replace. It all adds up to a lot more expense.

If you want to simplify your life and work less, then don't strap yourself down making hefty payments for a castle full of things you don't really need. Keep it simple. You'll have less stress. And more fun.

If you are already feeling trapped by a large house payment, maybe you should consider moving to a smaller home. Or perhaps refinancing your current loan will get your monthly payments reduced to a more manageable level. Doing so can significantly reduce your house payment, but determining whether it is right for you will take some homework. You will need to consider the costs involved in securing a new loan, whether or not you have a prepayment penalty on your current loan and how long you intend to stay in your home. Several Internet sites provide a free refinancing calculator to help you determine if it is best for you.

Education

Providing your children with a good education is one of your most important responsibilities. With a simplified lifestyle, you will have the time to carefully evaluate the choices available to your family and determine when, and where, formal education should begin. Of course, as the parent, you will be your children's most important educator, setting daily examples that will carry them throughout their life.

Preschool

If you and your spouse are working full time, you probably send your child to preschool or child care out of necessity. But if you simplified your family life and were able to work fewer hours or not at all, would you still need preschool? Even most nonworking parents send their little ones to preschool—if only for a few hours a week—to develop their group socialization skills. Other parents prefer to work closely with their little ones at home to assure kindergarten readiness. The book *Ready for Kindergarten* by Sharon Wilkins (Zondervan Publishing House, 2000) is a terrific source of activities that reinforce or introduce skills in preparation for kindergarten.

Public or Private?

The next decision in the education of your children is determining which school they will attend. Many parents prefer private or parochial school for a wide variety of good reasons, spending thousands of dollars a year per child in tuition. If the tuition is straining your finances, requiring both parents to work full time to pay for it, it may be time to seriously consider public schools instead. Are you choosing private or parochial schools because that's where all your friends send their children? Or because that's where you went as a child? Have you visited your public schools to see what they have to offer? If sending your children to public schools means you or your spouse could quit your job, perhaps you can work with your children at home to make up for anything you feel they are missing. Ask yourself if your child would be better off going to public school and having a parent at home.

If private or parochial school is the best place for your children, check into receiving financial assistance. Many schools offer scholarships or other forms of financial assistance, usually based on need, especially if you have more than one child attending. In addition, the National Association of Independent Schools, in Washington, D.C., can provide a list of organizations that offer financial support to help offset private school tuition.

After initiating some of the ideas presented in this book, you will, I hope, have more time to get involved at your children's school. I don't spend hours each week at school, but I do volunteer once a month in the computer lab and the cafeteria, and I attend the occasional field trip. That way I get to know my children's classmates, friends and teachers, making me better able to assess what is taking place while they are at school.

If your simplified family has Dad spending more hours at work than Mom, be sure to make time for Dad's involvement at school too. Studies show that kids with involved fathers do better in school than kids who have less-connected dads. They not only do better in academics, they are stronger social learners as well, feeling more satisfaction with school and friends.

Like private and parochial schools, public schools can have their share of expenses, too. Classroom fees, extracurricular activity fees, fund-raisers, school pictures, yearbooks, special tutors and book clubs are some of them. Some are mandatory, but others are optional. Remember, it's OK to say no.

Taxes

For most families, taxes eat up 20 percent or more of the family income. Unfortunately, for the most part, there is little you can do about it. But there are some useful places to look for savings. Keep in mind the following:

- Failing to carefully file your tax forms can cost you and your family extra money, money you'd surely rather spend on a vacation, a new car, or whatever your Wish List (Chapter 6) contains.

- In most cases, itemizing your deductions can keep taxes to a minimum. Current allowable deductions include:
  - State and local taxes
  - Charitable contributions including cash, clothing and furniture
  - Expenses related to your job
  - Medical and dental expenses, including mileage to and from the doctor

- — Casualty and theft losses
- — Tax planning advice and preparation
- — Cost of uniforms and cleaning those uniforms
- Although it will cost you, having a CPA prepare and file your tax forms may actually save you money. At my house, after years of struggling to file our own returns, we decided to pay a CPA. He found legitimate deductions we never considered, more than paying for the cost of his services.

Keeping track of deductions throughout the year is crucial if you intend to account for them on your tax return. We keep a folder in our file cabinet for the current year. Then, as we spend money on something that is deductible, we jot a note on the receipt as to what it was for and drop it in the folder. If we make a donation of clothing or furniture, we always ask for a receipt. At the end of the year, we gather our notes from the folder and also review our checkbook and credit card receipts for anything we may have missed. It's fairly simple and certainly worth the effort.

The simpler your lifestyle, the healthier your family budget. Using this chapter as your guide, identify the biggest drains on your family budget, then implement cost-saving changes like those suggested. The additional savings can be significant, providing you the opportunity to spend fewer hours at work and more hours at home with family doing the things you love most.

The Prices—A Simpler Family

It was the fall of 2000 when Ray and Beth Price decided it was time for a change. Ray had spent twenty-four of their twenty-six years of marriage in the military. His work was notable, but it meant frequent moves for the couple and their son Joseph. It was while living in Saudi Arabia, where Ray and Beth both worked at a major hospital, that the Prices made their decision. They had all the nice possessions of a well-to-do family. But long hours at work made for a lifestyle that was hectic, stressful, demanding and less than ideal for twelve-year-old Joseph.

After reevaluating their priorities, the family moved to Maine, where Beth accepted a good job with plenty of room for advancement. With Beth's support, Ray decided not to look for a job. Instead, he would stay home, take care of Joseph and the home front, and give Beth the opportunity to concentrate on her career. A quieter, calmer, simpler family life was the Prices' goal. But it wouldn't be easy. Their income decreased by $52,000 when Ray quit his job. To make it work without going into debt, the Prices set a weekly budget for groceries, Joseph's tuition, living expenses, savings and spending money. Now in a lower tax bracket, they would pay significantly less than the $30,000 they paid before Ray stopped working. "We actually have more money now, because we spend less than when we both worked. And we get to keep more of it due to the lower tax level," according to Ray.

With a smaller income, the Prices now concentrate on what they *need*, rather than what they *want*, and are thrilled with the outcome. They live in a 2,000-square-foot log home on four acres, instead of their previous 3,500-square-foot home (with a 900-square-foot finished basement) on an acre of perfectly manicured lawn. Ray recalls, "We used to spend $300 to $400 per month for electricity in the summer and four to five hours each weekend taking care of the lawn. For what? So we could say, 'Hey, look at how much money we can spend living in this house' "?

Joseph has adjusted to change. "He is not so wanting and understands why we sometimes aren't able to purchase everything he asks for," according to Ray. With his five-dollar weekly allowance Joseph has learned to save for the things that are important to him. And his grades have improved significantly thanks to more involvement from Dad.

Now, a typical day at the Price house has Mom and Dad up by 5:00 A.M. Ray makes breakfast and then drives Joseph and two neighbors to school by 7:30 A.M. Ray spends the school day doing typical household chores and making improvements to their log home (he recently enclosed the front porch). He picks up Joseph at 2:00, and then it's time for homework followed most days by swim team practice. The family enjoys dinner together each evening (which Ray usually prepares earlier in the day). The hectic commutes and hurried meals of their previous life are now replaced by pleasant afternoons and evenings as a family. "We have even found time to start walking again after dinner, something we haven't been able to do in years."

Ray says he may return to work again someday, "but only part time to help pay off the house so we could be totally free and independent of creditors." Their simpler arrangement is "working out just fine," he happily adds.

CHAPTER 9

Goals, Budget and Evaluation

"The tragedy of life is not that it ends so soon, but that we wait so long to begin it."

—W.M. Lewis

IN THE SPRING of 1993, I traded my full-time job for a less hectic, less stressful, lower-paying part-time job. When I did so, my family's combined annual income decreased by half—almost $40,000. But the quality of our lives increased more than I can say.

For a family that already lived fairly simply, finding ways to spend $40,000 less per year didn't seem easy. But after carefully looking at the numbers, I realized we didn't need to reduce our expenses by $40,000. As my income disappeared, I realized a lot of other costs would disappear, too. We would no longer need to pay for full-time child care, nice work clothes, or transportation to and from work five days a week. With a smaller family income, we would pay considerably less in taxes too. By working fewer hours, I would have the time to cook inexpensive meals for dinner instead of paying for carryout. And I would have the time to look for additional ways to reduce our expenses (all mentioned in this book).

Working fewer hours was my goal, but it may not be yours. Perhaps you would prefer to quit working altogether. Or maybe you want to continue working full time but are searching for ways to save money for college or other expenses. Perhaps you are motivated solely by a desire for a simpler, happier family.

This book is a collection of ideas that can add joy to your life. But when used together as part of a plan, the ideas in this book can make any of the goals mentioned a reality. This chapter shows how to follow three steps to becoming the simpler family you want to be:

1. Set a goal.
2. Develop a plan based on your current spending habits or use of time.
3. Evaluate your plan.

Set a Goal

Setting goals is like setting a direction for your life. Without a goal, your life can become a treadmill that never lets you off.

Meaningless activities—instead of activities that take you closer to where you want to be—become the norm. If you don't make it a goal to live more simply, the time and energy you might otherwise use to reach that goal will be used up by inconsequential activities instead, activities that take you further away from the simpler life you desire. You'll never get off the treadmill, and your life will never become less complicated.

By setting goals for yourself and your family, you'll achieve the following:

- Clarify what is most important to you and your spouse
- Know how much money it will take to achieve what is most important
- Know when to reasonably expect to achieve what is most important
- Avoid getting sidetracked spending time and money on things that are not important
- Realize that achieving your goals will suddenly become easier than you think

Get started thinking about your goals right now. Do you want to work forty hours instead of sixty, or twenty instead of forty, or not at all? Do you want to improve the quality and the quantity of your family time? Do you want to start a college fund for your children? Give yourself and your spouse a week to think about what is most important to you and your family. Determine exactly where you want to be headed. Individually write down your ideas, and prioritize them. Make a date with your spouse in a week to get together and compare notes. At this meeting, carefully consider the items on each other's list, adding and subtracting until you have an agreed-upon set of goals for your family's future.

Some goals are big and will require a lot of thought and effort to carry out. But the payoff of reaching such a goal can be tremendous, making it well worth the effort.

Develop a Plan

To avoid being sidetracked in your effort to reach your goals, you must establish a plan. Your plan is a series of carefully outlined steps that take you closer to your goal. Here is an example of a well-organized plan:

Goal

Quit my job to stay home with my children.

Steps to Take to Achieve My Goal

1. Determine how much my second income is actually contributing to the family income (see exercise later in this chapter).
2. Determine how much the family expenses need to be reduced to live without my income.
3. Put together a Spending/Saving Analysis (described later in this chapter) to determine where our money is currently being spent.
4. Determine which of our current expenses will be eliminated when I quit my job.
5. Using ideas in this book as a guide, target other expenses that can be reduced or eliminated to make my goal a reality.
6. Implement all expense-reduction ideas.
7. Quit job.

If your goal is to quit your job, or work fewer hours, it will be helpful to determine how much your current income is actually contributing to your family income. Determining the value of a second income is tricky. Below are two examples. As you'll see, there are many variables that come into play. For the sake of simplicity, these two scenarios make the following assumptions:

- The couple filed taxes jointly.
- The second income did not create additional tax deductions (like travel expenses) that would not exist otherwise.
- The couple has two children: ages three and six-months.
- The numbers reflect deductions as of 2001.

Family Number One

Dad makes $55,000.

After taking out the standard deduction of $7,600 and $11,600 in personal exemptions (that's $2,900 for each person in the family), Dad's taxable income is $35,800. If he were the only wage earner, the family would be in the 15 percent tax bracket and pay $5,370 in federal taxes. But he gets to deduct $500 per child as tax credits so will owe $4,370.

Mom makes $29,000.

All the family deductions were accounted for previously, so all of Mom's income is subject to federal income tax. Because of her salary, the family's taxable income is $64,800 (Dad's $35,800 plus Mom's $29,000). The combined incomes are in the 28 percent tax bracket. They must pay $12,268 in federal taxes, minus $500 per child tax credit. Total federal taxes due is $11,268. (Per the 2001 tax code, they pay 15 percent on the first $45,200 of taxable income and 28 percent on any taxable income above

$45,200). So instead of paying $4,370 in taxes, because of Mom's second income, the couple must pay an additional $6,898. If you subtract this additional amount of taxes from Mom's income, the value of her income is $22,102. But in addition to federal taxes, Mom also needs to pay Social Security, which is 6.25 percent of her salary; Medicare, which is 1.45 percent of her salary; approximately 5 percent in state tax; and possibly 2 percent in city tax. These additional taxes add up to 14.65 percent of her salary, or $4,249. Subtracting these additional taxes from $22,102 means the actual value of her $29,000 to her family is $17,853.

That's how much she is actually contributing to the family income.

Family Number Two

Mom makes $65,000.

After taking out the standard deduction of $7,600 and $11,600 in personal exemptions (that's $2,900 for each person in the family), Mom's taxable income is $45,800.

If she were the only wage earner, the family would pay 15 percent in taxes for the first $45,200 that Mom makes, and 28 percent in taxes for anything over that amount. In this scenario, Mom will pay $6,948 in taxes. After taking $500 per child tax credit, she will owe $5,948 in federal taxes.

Dad makes $50,000.

All the family deductions were accounted for previously, so all of Dad's income is subject to federal income tax. Because of his salary, the family's taxable income is $95,800 (mom's $45,800 plus dad's $50,000). The combined incomes are in the 28 percent tax bracket. They must pay $20,948 in taxes. (Per the 2001 tax code, they pay 15 percent on the first $45,200 of taxable income and 28 percent on any taxable income above $45,200). They still deduct $500 per child tax credit. So, instead of paying $5,948 in taxes, the couple is paying an additional $15,000. If you subtract this additional amount of taxes from Dad's income, the actual value of his income is $35,000. But Dad also needs to pay Social Security, Medicare, and state and city taxes, which add up to approximately 14.65 percent of his $50,000 salary, or $7,325. This means he is actually contributing $27,675 to the family income.

In both scenarios, because both parents work full time, the families have expenses they would not incur if one parent were at home. The biggest expense is for full-time child care. To determine the cost of such care, I phoned two reputable child-care centers in Cincinnati. The center with the lowest price for full-time care for a three-year-old and a six-month-old would charge $16,600 for a year. The older the child, the less it costs for full-time care.

If you deduct the cost of this full-time care from Mom's income in Family Number One, the family is left with $1,253.

If you deduct the price of this full-time child care from Dad's income in Family Number Two, the family is left with $11,075.

If either of these families wanted a parent to stay home instead of working, thus eliminating the need for child care, they could implement some of the cost-cutting measures outlined in this book to make it viable. In addition to the cost of child care, here are some other expenses they would no longer be paying:

- Gasoline to and from one job
- Dry cleaning one parent's work clothes
- Cost of new work clothes
- Lunches out with coworkers
- Holiday and birthday gifts for the boss and coworkers

When I left my full-time job to work part time, I considered "looking for ways to reduce expenses" as one of my new jobs. With the additional time and effort, it wasn't difficult to make ends meet. By following the advice outlined in earlier chapters, I'm guessing both of these families could find more ways to cut their expenses and make up for the lack of one income.

Where Is Your Money Currently Being Spent?

You now know how much you need to save in order to reach your goal. Before determining where you will make those savings, you will need to determine where your money is currently being spent. The steps outlined below will help you do so. Although taking the steps might be a bit tedious, the information you'll gain as a result will be valuable in many regards. Challenge everyone to be meticulous record keepers. Think of it as a fun activity that will take you closer to your family goals.

Step one in putting together a Spending/Savings Analysis is to determine exactly what your family expenses are right now. Maybe you think you already know. Complete the exercise anyway. I'm fairly certain you'll find one or two surprises. Without this step you won't be able to decide where adjustments can be made to more easily reach your goals. Here's what you need to do:

- Give everyone who spends the family income a small note-book (you, your spouse, any children old enough to spend your money).
- For the next month, insist that each of these persons record every single expense they have, including small purchases like a pack of gum or soda from a machine.
- Collect all receipts at the end of each day so that, if necessary, expenses can be broken down (your purchase at the gas station included a hot dog and soda as well as a tank of gas).
- Save the detailed invoice for any credit card bills that are paid during the month.

When the month has ended, break down all purchases into the following categories, indicating the amount spent in each category. Add categories that may be appropriate for your family.

Allowances for children	Gasoline
Car payment	Gifts
Charity	Groceries
Child care	Insurance
Clothing	Internet service provider
Credit card finance charges	Investments
Dry cleaner	Medical
Education	Phone
Entertainment	Rent/mortgage
Gas and electric	Restaurants

Savings

Snacks (convenience foods
   purchased outside the
   grocery store)

Taxes (other than those taken
   out of your paychecks)

Trash pickup

Water

Other (You don't want this to
   be an enormous amount.)

If you get billed quarterly for such things as real estate taxes, trash pickup, car insurance and water, estimate how much each costs on a monthly basis.

Step two in putting together your Spending/Saving Analysis is to determine your "after tax" family income for the same month. How much income does the family generate after taxes and Social Security are taken out?

Step three is comparing your income with your expenses.

- Do you have income left over after all expenses are paid? Good for you. You're living within your means.
- Do you have so much income left over that you could eliminate part (or all) of one income and still live comfortably, if that is your goal?
- Are your expenses significantly higher than your income? If so, it's time to put the ideas suggested throughout this book into place.

To simplify your life, ask yourself what can be reduced or eliminated to make your goal a reality? The advice in the earlier chapters of this book will guide you. Remember that cutting expenses is not the same as sacrificing. Trading a costly dinner in a fancy restaurant with an intimate family dinner around the kitchen table is not a "sacrifice." Refusing to purchase expensive designer-label clothing at the mall is not a sacrifice. Instead, you're giving up a dependence on labels and designers and other tools of the marketing industry in favor of casual, comfortable, quality, inexpensive clothing that is secondhand.

Your Spending/Saving Analysis will provide you the foundation for reducing expenses, adding to your savings, and reaching your family goals. Even purchases that seem insignificant will become routine and quickly add up. Do any of these scenarios sound familiar?

- Washing your car at home in the driveway is customary on Saturday mornings. Then one sunny day you spy a full-service hand car wash through your streaked windshield and decide to give your dirty car the works for eleven dollars. Next thing you know, you're spending forty-four dollars a month to keep your car clean.

- Borrowing videos from the library is standard practice at your house. One day you decide to treat your kids with a trip to Blockbuster. They are drunk with delight at all the choices. A few weeks later, you're a member of the "Frequent-Renter's Club."

- You purchase only store-brand cereals. But one day you have a coupon for Cinnamon-Flavored Life, which is already on sale, so you buy two boxes. Your daughter absolutely loves it, and now it appears regularly on your grocery list.

How Is Your Time Currently Being Spent?

Perhaps your goal is to find more time each day to spend with your family. To be successful, you will need to determine how you are spending your time right now. Like the spending exercise outlined previously, the Time Study outlined next takes careful effort. But the information you'll gain as a result will put your goal within easy reach.

To complete your Time Study, get a notebook small enough to carry with you at all times. For the next two weeks, record in your notebook everything you do and how much time it takes to do it. Your log should include everything from a five-minute chat with a friend or a walk with the dog to a dash into the grocery store. Be diligent about your Time Study, and don't skip a day.

After two weeks, it is time to carefully examine your time log, looking for the following:

- *Duplications.* How many trips did you make to the grocery store each week?
- *Similar tasks.* Did you visit the drug store, library, gas station and post office all in the same trip, or did you make four separate trips?
- *Multiple trips.* Are you making trips that aren't necessary? Are you shopping for items that could be ordered via the phone or Internet? Are your children's extracurricular activities, or your volunteer efforts, requiring more trips than you ever imagined?
- *Time spent waiting.* How much time did you spend waiting in the drive-through lane to order food? How long did you sit in traffic?

To simplify your life and make your goal a reality you must carefully examine your time log. What can be combined, reorganized or eliminated to make more time for family? Put together a plan for how you'll make more time based on the results of your time log. And before you take on a new commitment, ask yourself if it will take you further away from reaching your goal. Learn to say no. The advice in Chapter 1 will help you.

Keep Your Plan Visible

Once you have finalized your plan, write it down. Keep it visible. Make copies so you'll have one at work and one at home. Read your list often. Make a series of follow-up dates with your spouse to check on your progress.

Get Everyone Involved

As you get ready to implement your new plan, whether it be reducing your expenses or reducing time away from home, ask for the support of everyone in your family. What ideas can they contribute to ensure the plan's success? Everyone can have a hand in reducing expenses by questioning the real need behind each purchase before they make it. They can each play a part in reducing their time away from home by questioning their motivation before committing to another volunteer project, sports team or other outside activity. Remind everyone that time away can be disruptive to the entire family, not just to the individual involved in the activity.

Evaluate Your Plan

You've done your homework, made a plan, implemented it and reached your goal. Once a month, for the first few months, ask everyone if they are happy with the new arrangement. Overall, is everyone supportive? If not, how can you gain everyone's support without falling back into old habits? While ideally you want everyone's full approval, you may need to stand firm against some complaints if they are unreasonable (e.g., your teenage daughter wants more designer clothes than the new family budget can afford).

In spite of your best intentions, old habits sometimes have a way of creeping back into your routine: suddenly you're picking up a few groceries each week at the costlier "convenience store" instead of the supermarket where you regularly shop, or you start renting the newest, most expensive movies at the video store instead of borrowing from the library. You can prevent a step in the wrong direction and ensure long-term success by periodically evaluating your progress. Do another brief study of your spending patterns, or keep another brief time log. And look back at your original plan. Doing so will remind you of ideas you may have forgotten. Continue to search for new ideas as well. Search your library for books or magazines that teach the finer points of simple living. Talk with families that share your viewpoint. Hold firm. My guess is that you will be so happy with your new lifestyle that slipping back to your old habits will be incomprehensible.

Have the changes you've made resulted in more time with family, less stress, healthier eating habits? If not, find ways to adjust your plan so it does get you the results you want. As this book has shown, you will be rewarded with a more peaceful, more meaningful and happier family—a family that takes the time to appreciate the gifts they've been given and the time to fully explore what life has to offer, whose richness is measured in time and family, not money and possessions.

Resources

Complete Tightwad Gazette: Promoting Thrift as a Viable Alternative by Amy Dacyczyn (Random House, 1999)

Consumer Credit Counseling Service. If your family is seriously in debt and making only minimum payments on credit cards and other bills, contact the Consumer Credit Counseling Service in your area. This nationwide nonprofit service will help you negotiate with people you owe and put together a plan to eliminate your debt.

CHAPTER 10

Dealing with Common Obstacles and Things to Remember

"May you live every day of your life."

—Jonathan Swift

As you now understand, a simpler family life is within your reach. You undoubtedly are ready to begin living for today, instead of frantically working for a bigger house, a more expensive automobile or the most impressive investment portfolio. You no longer want to be counted among the 46 percent of Americans who work more than forty hours a week, or the 34 percent who work more than forty-five hours.

Common Obstacles

If you haven't already discovered it, you will soon realize that a more meaningful, enriching family life can be yours. It will become clear to you, as it did to me, that the rewards of a simpler family are tremendous. But as I learned when I went from a forty-hour to a twenty-hour workweek, the adjustments can have some pitfalls if you are not careful. Here are some common obstacles, with advice on how to deal with them.

Well-meaning family and friends don't want you to change your spending habits.

When family or friends suggest someplace expensive for dinner or entertainment, recommend a cheaper alternative. If they persist, remain cheerful, but tell them it's not in the budget right now. If you feel bad about missing out on a good time, remind yourself of everything you've gained as a result of your new habits. Don't try to keep up with the spending habits of others. Increase your circle of friends to include simpler families.

You get bombarded with fund-raisers.

When every child in the neighborhood stops by your house selling popcorn, wrapping paper, cookies, magazine subscriptions and raffle tickets, don't feel obligated. Smile and say, "Sorry, not this time."

Your frugal lifestyle becomes a source of amusement.

If people joke about your new spending philosophy, laugh along with them. Show them how much happier you can be without the burden of debt and with more free time to spend with your family.

Your children are feeling deprived because they can't fly to the beach for spring break, buy Nintendo or host elaborate birthday parties.

Simpler living provides parents an ideal opportunity to teach children to be smart consumers. A luxury item may be within their reach if they make it a goal and save for that goal. When they see an advertisement for something they just have to have, carefully explain how advertisements often exaggerate the truth and how the cost and benefits of an advertised item may not be as they appear. Likewise, talk to your children about peer pressure and how it affects buying behavior. Stress individuality instead. Take the time to comparison shop so your children can see for themselves the difference in cost and quality between a designer shirt at the mall, a lesser-known brand at a discount store and last year's fashions at a secondhand store. By helping your children set goals, analyze their options and comparison shop, you will help them develop valuable life skills.

When your children are feeling deprived, take the opportunity to talk, instead, about all the things for which you are grateful. Establish this bedtime routine: each night, just before lights out, everyone mentions three things for which they are thankful. By helping your family focus on what they have, in time they will spend less time thinking of the things they don't have.

Because you're spending more time at home, your house has suddenly become the gathering place for the neighborhood's unsupervised children.

It can be frustrating to find yourself supervising and refereeing not just your own children, but the children of neighbors who are happy to put you in charge—without pay. While it has its disadvantages (and you certainly need to speak up if these parents routinely take advantage of your availability), it has an up side as well. With the children under your wing, you're able to supervise their play, get to know their friends and keep an eye out for trouble. If it gets to be more than you can handle, you will want to take steps to limit the visits, but remember that it is better to have your children playing at their own house than to have them be unsupervised elsewhere.

Your simpler lifestyle enables you to become overinvolved in homework supervision.

Although you now have more time to pay close attention to your child's schoolwork, be careful not to get overinvolved. Ultimately, it is your child's responsibility to complete work on time and succeed in school. If you get too involved, your child may no longer feel ownership, instead blaming you when his grades aren't as good as you expect.

Things to Remember

When making the transition to being a simpler family, there are a few things to keep in mind that will make the process smoother.

Don't burn your bridges.

If you're leaving your current place of employment, don't announce to your coworkers that you "hate this place and can't wait to get out of here." Be gracious. Your relationship with your former employer may be vital to a new career someday.

Do make it a point to do something special with your little ones when they are home with you.

You've been given a tremendous gift—the gift of time with your children. Appreciate that gift, and make every day you are home with them special by doing something fun. Soon they will be off to school, and the opportunity will be gone.

Before my children were in school full time, we spent many an afternoon sitting on a bench outside the neighborhood bakery, sharing a doughnut and watching the school buses go by. Then ages four and two, the kids would chatter excitedly about what it would be like to someday ride the bus with the "big kids." Today, in the blink of an eye, they are those big kids. But they still reminisce about our afternoons on the bench, faces full of chocolate icing, watching the buses go by.

Don't be obsessed with a clean house.

You didn't come this far to spend your days cleaning house while your children park themselves in front of the television. As my friend Donna told me just the other day when our boys tracked muddy boots through her family room, "It's only dirt!"

Don't fill your new free time with volunteer activities for at least the first six months.

Once word gets out that you're home more often, you'll be deluged with requests to volunteer your time on school, church or charity projects. Refuse all requests for at least six months. You need that time, instead, to determine how to effectively juggle the responsibilities of family and household. And you certainly don't want your little ones to end up with baby-sitters all day while you're out volunteering.

Do make it your job to ensure that your family lives within your new budget.

If your simpler lifestyle has meant a reduction in family income, make it your responsibility to see that you have reduced your expenses accordingly. Initially, the adjustment will require careful attention to be sure you don't slide back to your old spending habits.

Don't limit socializing only to parents of children the same ages as your own.

You don't want to become one of those parents that other people dread—able to talk endlessly about your children and nothing else. Join a reading group, attend lectures, take a class or become an advocate for family-friendly programming. Use your time to rediscover old interests or develop new ones. The entire family will be rewarded.

Do expand your circle of friends to include like-minded people who also advocate simpler living.

Share your ideas and challenges about your simpler lifestyle with them, and ask that they do the same. Read books and magazines that support your new lifestyle. They will remind you of the many ways your efforts have enriched your family. And they will provide you new ideas for continuing to do so.

Do spend quiet time exploring your spiritual side.

Regularly search for things that make you feel fulfilled and content. Be conscious of your ability to begin a new career in the future, or to follow a new path. Keep your eyes open, and eventually you will know exactly what you want to do.

Do search for ways to stimulate the minds of your young ones.

The questions you ask, the conversations you encourage and the activities you initiate can all have a profound effect on their development. Search your library for books to guide you and your children. Their future success in school may be due, in large part, to the things you do with them when they are young.

Don't become your children's entertainment director now that you have more time to do so.

Remember that ultimately you want your children to become self-sufficient, which will not happen if they rely on you to keep them busy every minute of the day.

Above all else, do not lose sight of your goal of being a simpler, calmer and happier family. Remind yourself that life is not a race to a finish line where you will one day find complete happiness. Instead, make the change to a simpler family life and understand that complete happiness can be a reality today. Take control, make the necessary changes and start living.

About the Author

CHRISTINE KLEIN is married and the mother of two. She left a successful marketing career to pursue her dream of living her life on her own terms, by working less and spending more time with her family. This book is the product of the strategy she created to accomplish that. Now a marketing consultant and freelance writer with plenty of time for her family and herself, she lives in Cincinnati, Ohio.